**HBR'S
10
MUST
READS**

On
**Managing Across
Cultures**

HBR's 10 Must Reads series is the definitive collection of ideas and best practices for aspiring and experienced leaders alike. These books offer essential reading selected from the pages of *Harvard Business Review* on topics critical to the success of every manager.

Titles include:

HBR's 10 Must Reads 2015
HBR's 10 Must Reads 2016
HBR's 10 Must Reads on Change Management
HBR's 10 Must Reads on Collaboration
HBR's 10 Must Reads on Communication
HBR's 10 Must Reads on Emotional Intelligence
HBR's 10 Must Reads on Innovation
HBR's 10 Must Reads on Leadership
HBR's 10 Must Reads on Making Smart Decisions
HBR's 10 Must Reads on Managing Across Cultures
HBR's 10 Must Reads on Managing People
HBR's 10 Must Reads on Managing Yourself
HBR's 10 Must Reads on Strategic Marketing
HBR's 10 Must Reads on Strategy
HBR's 10 Must Reads on Teams
HBR's 10 Must Reads: The Essentials

HBR'S 10 MUST READS

On
Managing
Across
Cultures

HARVARD BUSINESS REVIEW PRESS

Boston, Massachusetts

Library of Congress Cataloging-in-Publication Data

Names: Harvard Business Review Press, issuing body.
   Title: HBR's 10 must reads on managing across cultures / Harvard Business Review Press.
Description: Boston, Massachusetts : Harvard Business Review Press, [2016] | Includes index.
Identifiers: LCCN 2015047174 (print) | LCCN 2016003334 (ebook) | ISBN 9781633694613 | ISBN 9781633691636 ()
Subjects: LCSH: International business enterprises—Personnel management. | Management—Cross-cultural studies. | Corporate culture—Cross-cultural studies. | Diversity in the workplace—Management.
Classific ation: LCC HF5549.5.E45 H423 2016 (print) | LCC HF5549.5.E45 (ebook) | DDC 658.3008—dc23
LC record available at http://lccn.loc.gov/2015047174

ISBN: 978-1-63369-461-3
eISBN:978-1-63369-163-6

Contents

**HBR'S
10
MUST
READS**

On
**Managing Across
Cultures**

Cultural Intelligence

by P. Christopher Earley and Elaine Mosakowski

YOU SEE THEM AT INTERNATIONAL airports like Heathrow: posters advertising the global bank HSBC that show a grasshopper and the message "USA—Pest. China—Pet. Northern Thailand—Appetizer."

Taxonomists pinned down the scientific definition of the family Acrididae more than two centuries ago. But culture is so powerful it can affect how even a lowly insect is perceived. So it should come as no surprise that the human actions, gestures, and speech patterns a person encounters in a foreign business setting are subject to an even wider range of interpretations, including ones that can make misunderstandings likely and cooperation impossible. But occasionally an outsider has a seemingly natural ability to interpret someone's unfamiliar and ambiguous gestures in just the way that person's compatriots and colleagues would, even to mirror them. We call that *cultural intelligence* or *CQ*. In a world where crossing boundaries is routine, CQ becomes a vitally important aptitude and skill, and not just for international bankers and borrowers.

Companies, too, have cultures, often very distinctive; anyone who joins a new company spends the first few weeks deciphering its cultural code. Within any large company there are sparring subcultures as well: The sales force can't talk to the engineers, and the PR people lose patience with the lawyers. Departments, divisions, professions, geographical regions—each has a constellation of manners, meanings, histories, and values that will confuse the interloper and cause him or her to stumble. Unless, that is, he or she has a high CQ.

Cultural intelligence is related to emotional intelligence, but it picks up where emotional intelligence leaves off. A person with high emotional intelligence grasps what makes us human and at the same time what makes each of us different from one another. A person with high cultural intelligence can somehow tease out of a person's or group's behavior those features that would be true of all people and all groups, those peculiar to this person or this group, and those that are neither universal nor idiosyncratic. The vast realm that lies between those two poles is culture.

An American expatriate manager we know had his cultural intelligence tested while serving on a design team that included two German engineers. As other team members floated their ideas, the engineers condemned them repeatedly as stunted or immature or worse. The manager concluded that Germans in general are rude and aggressive.

A modicum of cultural intelligence would have helped the American realize he was mistakenly equating the merit of an idea with the merit of the person presenting it and that the Germans were able to make a sharp distinction between the two. A manager with even subtler powers of discernment might have tried to determine how much of the two Germans' behavior was arguably German and how much was explained by the fact that they were engineers.

An expatriate manager who was merely emotionally intelligent would probably have empathized with the team members whose ideas were being criticized, modulated his or her spontaneous reaction to the engineers' conduct, and proposed a new style of discussion that preserved candor but spared feelings, if indeed anyone's feelings had been hurt. But without being able to tell how much of the engineers' behavior was idiosyncratic and how much was culturally determined, he or she would not have known how to influence their actions or how easy it would be to do that.

One critical element that cultural intelligence and emotional intelligence do share is, in psychologist Daniel Goleman's words, "a propensity to suspend judgment—to think before acting." For someone richly endowed with CQ, the suspension might take hours or days, while someone with low CQ might have to take weeks or months. In either case, it involves using your senses to register all

Idea in Brief

In an increasingly diverse business environment, managers must be able to navigate through the thicket of habits, gestures, and assumptions that define their coworkers' differences. Foreign cultures are everywhere—in other countries, certainly, but also in corporations, vocations, and regions. Interacting with individuals within them demands perceptiveness and adaptability. And the people who have those traits in abundance aren't necessarily the ones who enjoy the greatest social success in familiar settings. Cultural intelligence, or CQ, is the ability to make sense of unfamiliar contexts and then blend in. It has three components—the cognitive, the physical, and the emotional/

motivational. While it shares many of the properties of emotional intelligence, CQ goes one step further by equipping a person to distinguish behaviors produced by the culture in question from behaviors that are peculiar to particular individuals and those found in all human beings. In their surveys of 2,000 managers in 60 countries, the authors found that most managers are not equally strong in all three of these areas of cultural intelligence. The authors have devised tools that show how to identify one's strengths, and they have developed training techniques to help people overcome weaknesses. They conclude that anyone reasonably alert, motivated, and poised can attain an acceptable CQ.

the ways that the personalities interacting in front of you are different from those in your home culture yet similar to one another. Only when conduct you have actually observed begins to settle into patterns can you safely begin to anticipate how these people will react in the next situation. The inferences you draw in this manner will be free of the hazards of stereotyping.

The people who are socially the most successful among their peers often have the greatest difficulty making sense of, and then being accepted by, cultural strangers. Those who fully embody the habits and norms of their native culture may be the most alien when they enter a culture not their own. Sometimes, people who are somewhat detached from their own culture can more easily adopt the mores and even the body language of an unfamiliar host. They're used to being observers and making a conscious effort to fit in.

Although some aspects of cultural intelligence are innate, anyone reasonably alert, motivated, and poised can attain an acceptable level of cultural intelligence, as we have learned from surveying 2,000 managers in 60 countries and training many others. Given the number of cross-functional assignments, job transfers, new employers, and distant postings most corporate managers are likely to experience in the course of a career, low CQ can turn out to be an inherent disadvantage.

The Three Sources of Cultural Intelligence

Can it really be that some managers are socially intelligent in their own settings but ineffective in culturally novel ones? The experience of Peter, a sales manager at a California medical devices group acquired by Eli Lilly Pharmaceuticals, is not unusual. At the devices company, the atmosphere had been mercenary and competitive; the best-performing employees could make as much in performance bonuses as in salary. Senior managers hounded unproductive salespeople to perform better.

At Lilly's Indianapolis headquarters, to which Peter was transferred, the sales staff received bonuses that accounted for only a small percentage of total compensation. Furthermore, criticism was restrained and confrontation kept to a minimum. To motivate people, Lilly management encouraged them. Peter commented, "Back in L.A., I knew how to handle myself and how to manage my sales team. I'd push them and confront them if they weren't performing, and they'd respond. If you look at my evaluations, you'll see that I was very successful and people respected me. Here in Indianapolis, they don't like my style, and they seem to avoid the challenges that I put to them. I just can't seem to get things done as well here as I did in California."

Peter's problem was threefold. First, he didn't comprehend how much the landscape had changed. Second, he was unable to make his behavior consistent with that of everyone around him. And third, when he recognized that the arrangement wasn't working, he became disheartened.

Peter's three difficulties correspond to the three components of cultural intelligence: the cognitive; the physical; and the emotional/ motivational. Cultural intelligence resides in the body and the heart, as well as the head. Although most managers are not equally strong in all three areas, each faculty is seriously hampered without the other two.

Head

Rote learning about the beliefs, customs, and taboos of foreign cultures, the approach corporate training programs tend to favor, will never prepare a person for every situation that arises, nor will it prevent terrible gaffes. However, inquiring about the meaning of some custom will often prove unavailing because natives may be reticent about explaining themselves to strangers, or they may have little practice looking at their own culture analytically.

Instead, a newcomer needs to devise what we call learning strategies. Although most people find it difficult to discover a point of entry into alien cultures, whose very coherence can make them seem like separate, parallel worlds, an individual with high cognitive CQ notices clues to a culture's shared understandings. These can appear in any form and any context but somehow indicate a line of interpretation worth pursuing.

An Irish manager at an international advertising firm was working with a new client, a German construction and engineering company. Devin's experience with executives in the German retail clothing industry was that they were reasonably flexible about deadlines and receptive to highly imaginative proposals for an advertising campaign. He had also worked with executives of a British construction and engineering company, whom he found to be strict about deadlines and intent on a media campaign that stressed the firm's technical expertise and the cost savings it offered.

Devin was unsure how to proceed. Should he assume that the German construction company would take after the German clothing retailer or, instead, the British construction company? He resolved to observe the new client's representative closely and draw general conclusions about the firm and its culture from his behavior, just as he had done in the other two cases. Unfortunately, the client sent a new representative to every meeting. Many came from different business units and had grown up in different countries. Instead of equating the first representative's behavior with the client's corporate culture, Devin looked for consistencies in the various individuals' traits. Eventually he determined that they were all punctual, deadline-oriented, and tolerant of unconventional advertising messages. From that, he was able to infer much about the character of their employer.

Body

You will not disarm your foreign hosts, guests, or colleagues simply by showing you understand their culture; your actions and demeanor must prove that you have already to some extent entered their world. Whether it's the way you shake hands or order a coffee, evidence of an ability to mirror the customs and gestures of the people around you will prove that you esteem them well enough to want to be like them. By adopting people's habits and mannerisms, you eventually come to understand in the most elemental way what it is like to be them. They, in turn, become more trusting and open. University of Michigan professor Jeffrey Sanchez-Burks's research on cultural barriers in business found that job candidates who adopted some of the mannerisms of recruiters with cultural backgrounds different from their own were more likely to be made an offer.

This won't happen if a person suffers from a deep-seated reservation about the called-for behavior or lacks the physical poise to pull it off. Henri, a French manager at Aegis, a media corporation, followed the national custom of greeting his female clients with a hug and a kiss on both cheeks. Although Melanie, a British aerospace manager, understood that in France such familiarity was de rigueur in a professional setting, she couldn't suppress her discomfort when it happened to her, and she recoiled. Inability to receive and reciprocate gestures that are culturally characteristic reflects a low level of cultural intelligence's physical component.

In another instance, a Hispanic community leader in Los Angeles and an Anglo-American businessman fell into conversation at a charity event. As the former moved closer, the latter backed away. It took nearly 30 minutes of waltzing around the room for the community leader to realize that "Anglos" were not comfortable standing in such close physical proximity.

Heart

Adapting to a new culture involves overcoming obstacles and setbacks. People can do that only if they believe in their own efficacy. If they persevered in the face of challenging situations in the past, their confidence grew. Confidence is always rooted in mastery of a particular task or set of circumstances.

A person who doesn't believe herself capable of understanding people from unfamiliar cultures will often give up after her efforts meet with hostility or incomprehension. By contrast, a person with high motivation will, upon confronting obstacles, setbacks, or even failure, reengage with greater vigor. To stay motivated, highly efficacious people do not depend on obtaining rewards, which may be unconventional or long delayed.

Hyong Moon had experience leading racially mixed teams of designers at GM, but when he headed up a product design and development team that included representatives from the sales, production, marketing, R&D, engineering, and finance departments, things did not go smoothly. The sales manager, for example, objected to the safety engineer's attempt to add features such as side-impact air bags because they would boost the car's price excessively. The conflict became so intense and so public that a senior manager had to intervene. Although many managers would have felt chastened after that, Moon struggled even harder to gain control, which he eventually did by convincing the sales manager that the air bags could make the car more marketable. Although he had no experience with cross-functional teams, his successes with single-function teams had given him the confidence to persevere. He commented, "I'd seen these types of disagreements in other teams, and I'd been able to help team members overcome their differences, so I knew I could do it again."

How Head, Body, and Heart Work Together

At the end of 1997, U.S.-based Merrill Lynch acquired UK-based Mercury Asset Management. At the time of the merger, Mercury was a decorous, understated, hierarchical company known for doing business in the manner of an earlier generation. Merrill, by contrast, was informal, fast-paced, aggressive, and entrepreneurial. Both companies had employees of many nationalities. Visiting Mercury about six months after the merger announcement, we were greeted by Chris, a Mercury personnel manager dressed in khakis and a knit shirt. Surprised by the deviation from his usual uniform of gray or navy pinstripes, we asked him what had happened. He told

Diagnosing Your Cultural Intelligence

THESE STATEMENTS REFLECT DIFFERENT facets of cultural intelligence. For each set, add up your scores and divide by four to produce an average. Our work with large groups of managers shows that for purposes of your own development, it is most useful to think about your three scores in comparison to one another. Generally, an average of less than 3 would indicate an area calling for improvement, while an average of greater than 4.5 reflects a true CQ strength.

Rate the extent to which you agree with each statement, using the scale:

1 = strongly disagree, 2 = disagree, 3 = neutral, 4 = agree, 5 = strongly agree.

_____ Before I interact with people from a new culture, I ask myself what I hope to achieve.

_____ If I encounter something unexpected while working in a new culture, I use this experience to figure out new ways to approach *other* cultures in the future.

_____ I plan how I'm going to relate to people from a different culture before I meet them.

+ _____ When I come into a new cultural situation, I can immediately sense whether something is going well or something is wrong.

Total _____ ÷ 4 = ☐ Cognitive CQ

---

us that Merrill had instituted casual Fridays in its own offices and then extended the policy on a volunteer basis to its UK sites.

Chris understood the policy as Merrill's attempt to reduce hierarchical distinctions both within and between the companies. The intention, he thought, was to draw the two enterprises closer together. Chris also identified a liking for casual dress as probably an American cultural trait.

Not all Mercury managers were receptive to the change, however. Some went along with casual Fridays for a few weeks, then gave up. Others never doffed their more formal attire, viewing the new policy as a victory of carelessness over prudence and an attempt by Merrill to impose its identity on Mercury, whose professional

It's easy for me to change my body language (for example, eye contact or posture) to suit people from a different culture.

_____

I can alter my expression when a cultural encounter requires it.

_____

I modify my speech style (for example, accent or tone) to suit people from a different culture.

_____

I easily change the way I act when a cross-cultural encounter seems to require it.

+ _____

Total   _____ ÷ 4 = ☐ **Physical CQ**

I have confidence that I can deal well with people from a different culture.

_____

I am certain that I can befriend people whose cultural backgrounds are different from mine.

_____

I can adapt to the lifestyle of a different culture with relative ease.

_____

I am confident that I can deal with a cultural situation that's unfamiliar.

+ _____

Total   _____ ÷ 4 = ☐ **Emotional/motivational CQ**

dignity would suffer as a result. In short, the Mercury resisters did not understand the impulse behind the change (head); they could not bring themselves to alter their appearance (body); and they had been in the Mercury environment for so long that they lacked the motivation (heart) to see the experiment through. To put it even more simply, they dreaded being mistaken for Merrill executives.

How would you behave in a similar situation? The sidebar "Diagnosing Your Cultural Intelligence" allows you to assess the three facets of your own cultural intelligence and learn where your relative strengths and weaknesses lie. Attaining a high absolute score is not the objective.

Cultural Intelligence Profiles

Most managers fit at least one of the following six profiles. By answering the questions in the exhibit, you can decide which one describes you best.

The provincial can be quite effective when working with people of similar background but runs into trouble when venturing farther afield. A young engineer at Chevrolet's truck division received positive evaluations of his technical abilities as well as his interpersonal skills. Soon he was asked to lead a team at Saturn, an autonomous division of GM. He was not able to adjust to Saturn's highly participative approach to teamwork—he mistakenly assumed it would be as orderly and deferential as Chevy's. Eventually, he was sent back to Chevy's truck division.

The analyst methodically deciphers a foreign culture's rules and expectations by resorting to a variety of elaborate learning strategies. The most common form of analyst realizes pretty quickly he is in alien territory but then ascertains, usually in stages, the nature of the patterns at work and how he should interact with them. Deirdre, for example, works as a broadcast director for a London-based company. Her principal responsibility is negotiating contracts with broadcast media owners. In June 2002, her company decided that all units should adopt a single negotiating strategy, and it was Deirdre's job to make sure this happened. Instead of forcing a showdown with the managers who resisted, she held one-on-one meetings in which she probed their reasons for resisting, got them together to share ideas, and revised the negotiating strategy to incorporate approaches they had found successful. The revised strategy was more culturally flexible than the original proposal—and the managers chose to cooperate.

The natural relies entirely on his intuition rather than on a systematic learning style. He is rarely steered wrong by first impressions. Donald, a brand manager for Unilever, commented, "As part of my job, I need to judge people from a wide variety of cultural backgrounds and understand their needs quickly. When I come into a new situation, I watch everyone for a few minutes and then I get a general sense of what is going on and how I need to act. I'm not really sure how I do it, but it seems to work." When facing ambiguous multicultural situations that he must take control of, the natural may falter because he has never had to improvise learning strategies or cope with feelings of disorientation.

The ambassador, like many political appointees, may not know much about the culture he has just entered, but he convincingly communicates his certainty that he belongs there. Among the managers of multinational companies we have studied, the ambassador is the most common type. His confidence is a very powerful component of his cultural intelligence. Some of it may be derived from watching how other managers have succeeded in comparable situations. The ambassador must have the humility to know what he doesn't know—that is, to know how to avoid underestimating cultural differences, even though doing so will inflict a degree of discomfort.

The mimic has a high degree of control over his actions and behavior, if not a great deal of insight into the significance of the cultural cues he picks up. Mimicry definitely puts hosts and guests at ease, facilitates communication, and builds trust. Mimicry is not, however, the same as pure imitation, which can be interpreted as mocking. Ming, a manager at the Shanghai regional power authority, relates, "When I deal with foreigners, I try to adopt their style of speaking and interacting. I find that simple things like keeping the right distance from the other person or making eye contact or speaking English at a speed that matches the other person's puts them at ease and makes it easier to make a connection. This really makes a difference to newcomers to China because they often are a bit threatened by the place."

The chameleon possesses high levels of all three CQ components and is a very uncommon managerial type. He or she even may be mistaken for a native of the country. More important, chameleons don't generate any of the ripples that unassimilated foreigners inevitably do. Some are able to achieve results that natives cannot, due to their insider's skills and outsider's perspective. We found that only about 5% of the managers we surveyed belonged in this remarkable category.

One of them is Nigel, a British entrepreneur who has started businesses in Australia, France, and Germany. The son of diplomats, Nigel grew up all over the world. Most of his childhood, however, was spent in Saudi Arabia. After several successes of his own, some venture capitalists asked him to represent them in dealings with the founder of a money-losing Pakistani start-up.

To the founder, his company existed chiefly to employ members of his extended family and, secondarily, the citizens of Lahore. The VCs, naturally, had a different idea. They were tired of losses and wanted Nigel to persuade the founder to close down the business.

Upon relocating to Lahore, Nigel realized that the interests of family and community were not aligned. So he called in several community leaders, who agreed to meet with managers and try to convince them that the larger community of Lahore would be hurt if potential investors came to view it as full of businesspeople unconcerned with a company's solvency. Nigel's Saudi upbringing had made him aware of Islamic principles of personal responsibility to the wider community, while his British origins tempered what in another person's hands might have been the mechanical application of those tenets. Throughout the negotiations, he displayed an authoritative style appropriate to the Pakistani setting. In relatively short order, the managers and the family agreed to terminate operations.

Many managers, of course, are a hybrid of two or more of the types. We discovered in our survey of more than 2,000 managers that even more prevalent than the ambassador was a hybrid of that type and the analyst. One example was a female African-American manager in Cairo named Brenda, who was insulted when a small group of young, well-meaning Egyptian males greeted her with a phrase they'd learned from rap music.

"I turned on my heel, went right up to the group and began upbraiding them as strongly as my Arabic would allow," she said. "When I'd had my say, I stormed off to meet a friend."

"After I had walked about half a block, I registered the shocked look on their faces as they listened to my words. I then realized they must have thought they were greeting me in a friendly way. So I went back to talk to the group. They asked me why I was so angry, I explained, they apologized profusely, and we all sat down and had tea and an interesting talk about how the wrong words can easily cause trouble. During our conversation, I brought up a number of examples of how Arabic expressions uttered in the wrong way or by the wrong person could spark an equivalent reaction in them. After spending about an hour with them, I had some new friends."

Brenda's narrative illustrates the complexities and the perils of cross-cultural interactions. The young men had provoked her by trying, ineptly, to ingratiate themselves by using a bit of current slang from her native land. Forgetting in her anger that she was the stranger, she berated them for what was an act of cultural ignorance, not malice. Culturally uninformed mimicry got the young men in trouble; Brenda's—and the men's—cognitive flexibility and willingness to reengage got them out of it.

Cultivating Your Cultural Intelligence

Unlike other aspects of personality, cultural intelligence can be developed in psychologically healthy and professionally competent people. In our work with Deutsche Bank, we introduced a program to improve managers' work relationships with outsourcing partners in India. We developed a two-and-a-half day program that first identified a participant's strengths and weaknesses and then provided a series of steps, which we outline below, to enhance their CQ.

Step 1

The individual examines his CQ strengths and weaknesses in order to establish a starting point for subsequent development efforts. Our self-assessment instrument is one approach, but there are others, such as an assessment of a person's behavior in a simulated business encounter and 360-degree feedback on a person's past behavior in an actual situation. Hughes Electronics, for example, staged a cocktail party to evaluate an expatriate manager's grasp of South Korean social etiquette. Ideally, a manager will undergo a variety of assessments.

Step 2

The person selects training that focuses on her weaknesses. For example, someone lacking physical CQ might enroll in acting classes. Someone lacking cognitive CQ might work on developing his analogical and inductive reasoning—by, for example, reading several business case studies and distilling their common principles.

Step 3

The general training set out above is applied. If motivational CQ is low, a person might be given a series of simple exercises to perform, such as finding out where to buy a newspaper or greeting someone who has arrived to be interviewed. Mastering simple activities such as greetings or transactions with local shopkeepers establishes a solid base from which to move into more demanding activities, such as giving an employee a performance appraisal.

Step 4

The individual organizes her personal resources to support the approach she has chosen. Are there people at her organization with the skills to conduct this training, and does her work unit provide support for it? A realistic assessment of her workload and the time available for CQ enhancement is important.

Step 5

The person enters the cultural setting he needs to master. He coordinates his plans with others, basing them on his CQ strengths and remaining weaknesses. If his strength is mimicry, for example, he would be among the first in his training group to venture forth. If his strength is analysis, he would first want to observe events unfold and then explain to the others why they followed the pattern they did.

Step 6

The individual reevaluates her newly developed skills and how effective they have been in the new setting, perhaps after collecting

Confidence Training

HELMUT WAS A MANAGER at a Berlin-based high-tech company who participated in our cultural-intelligence training program at London Business School. Three months earlier, he had been assigned to a large manufacturing facility in southern Germany to supervise the completion of a new plant and guide the local staff through the launch. Helmut came from northern Germany and had never worked in southern Germany; his direct reports had been raised in southern Germany and had worked for the local business unit for an average of seven years.

Helmut was good at developing new learning strategies, and he wasn't bad at adapting his behavior to his surroundings. But he had low confidence in his ability to cope with his new colleagues. To him, southern Germans were essentially foreigners; he found them "loud, brash, and cliquish."

To capitalize on his resourcefulness and build his confidence, we placed Helmut in heterogeneous groups of people, whom we encouraged to engage in freewheeling discussions. We also encouraged him to express his emotions more openly, in the manner of his southern compatriots, and to make more direct eye contact in the course of role-playing exercises.

Helmut's resourcefulness might have impelled him to take on more ambitious tasks than he could quite handle. It was important he get his footing first, so that some subsequent reversal would not paralyze him. To enhance his motivational CQ, we asked him to list ten activities he thought would be part of his daily or weekly routine when he returned to Munich.

By the time Helmut returned to London for his second training session, he had proved to himself he could manage simple encounters like getting a coffee, shopping, and having a drink with colleagues. So we suggested he might be ready for more challenging tasks, such as providing face-to-face personnel appraisals. Even though Helmut was skilled at analyzing people's behavior, he doubted he was equal to this next set of hurdles. We encouraged him to view his analytic skills as giving him an important advantage. For example, Helmut had noticed that Bavarians were extroverted only with people familiar to them. With strangers they could be as formal as any Prussian. Realizing this allowed him to respond flexibly to either situation instead of being put off balance.

By the time he was asked to lead a quality-improvement team, he had concluded that his leadership style must unfold in two stages—commanding at the outset, then more personal and inclusive. On his third visit to London, Helmut reported good relations with the quality improvement team, and the members corroborated his assessment.

360-degree feedback from colleagues individually or eavesdropping on a casual focus group that was formed to discuss her progress. She may decide to undergo further training in specific areas.

In the sidebar "Confidence Training," we describe how we applied these six steps to the case of Helmut, one of five German managers we helped at their employer's behest as they coped with new assignments within and outside of Germany.

———————

Why can some people act appropriately and effectively in new cultures or among people with unfamiliar backgrounds while others flounder? Our anecdotal and empirical evidence suggests that the answer doesn't lie in tacit knowledge or in emotional or social intelligence. But a person with high CQ, whether cultivated or innate, can understand and master such situations, persevere, and do the right thing when needed.

Originally published in October 2004. Reprint R0410J

Managing Multicultural Teams

by Jeanne Brett, Kristin Behfar, and Mary C. Kern

WHEN A MAJOR INTERNATIONAL SOFTWARE developer needed to produce a new product quickly, the project manager assembled a team
of employees from India and the United States. From the start the
team members could not agree on a delivery date for the product.
The Americans thought the work could be done in two to three
weeks; the Indians predicted it would take two to three months. As
time went on, the Indian team members proved reluctant to report
setbacks in the production process, which the American team members would find out about only when work was due to be passed to
them. Such conflicts, of course, may affect any team, but in this case
they arose from cultural differences. As tensions mounted, conflict
over delivery dates and feedback became personal, disrupting team
members' communication about even mundane issues. The project
manager decided he had to intervene—with the result that both the
American and the Indian team members came to rely on him for direction regarding minute operational details that the team should
have been able to handle itself. The manager became so bogged
down by quotidian issues that the project careened hopelessly off
even the most pessimistic schedule—and the team never learned to
work together effectively.

Multicultural teams often generate frustrating management
dilemmas. Cultural differences can create substantial obstacles to

effective teamwork—but these may be subtle and difficult to recognize until significant damage has already been done. As in the case above, which the manager involved told us about, managers may create more problems than they resolve by intervening. The challenge in managing multicultural teams effectively is to recognize underlying cultural causes of conflict, and to intervene in ways that both get the team back on track and empower its members to deal with future challenges themselves.

We interviewed managers and members of multicultural teams from all over the world. These interviews, combined with our deep research on dispute resolution and teamwork, led us to conclude that the wrong kind of managerial intervention may sideline valuable members who should be participating or, worse, create resistance, resulting in poor team performance. We're not talking here about respecting differing national standards for doing business, such as accounting practices. We're referring to day-to-day working problems among team members that can keep multicultural teams from realizing the very gains they were set up to harvest, such as knowledge of different product markets, culturally sensitive customer service, and 24-hour work rotations.

The good news is that cultural challenges are manageable if managers and team members choose the right strategy and avoid imposing single-culture-based approaches on multicultural situations.

The Challenges

People tend to assume that challenges on multicultural teams arise from differing styles of communication. But this is only one of the four categories that, according to our research, can create barriers to a team's ultimate success. These categories are direct versus indirect communication; trouble with accents and fluency; differing attitudes toward hierarchy and authority; and conflicting norms for decision making.

Direct versus indirect communication
Communication in Western cultures is typically direct and explicit. The meaning is on the surface, and a listener doesn't have to know

Idea in Brief

If your company does business internationally, you're probably leading teams with members from diverse cultural backgrounds. Those differences can present serious obstacles. For example, some members' lack of fluency in the team's dominant language can lead others to underestimate their competence. When such obstacles arise, your team can stalemate.

To get the team moving again, avoid intervening directly, advise Brett, Behfar, and Kern. Though sometimes necessary, your involvement can prevent team members from solving problems themselves—and learning from that process.

Instead, choose one of three indirect interventions. When possible, encourage team members to **adapt** by acknowledging cultural gaps and working around them. If your team isn't able to be open about their differences, consider **structural intervention** (e.g., reassigning members to reduce interpersonal friction). As a last resort, use an **exit** strategy (e.g., removing a member from the team).

There's no one right way to tackle multicultural problems. But understanding four barriers to team success can help you begin evaluating possible responses.

much about the context or the speaker to interpret it. This is not true in many other cultures, where meaning is embedded in the way the message is presented. For example, Western negotiators get crucial information about the other party's preferences and priorities by asking direct questions, such as "Do you prefer option A or option B?" In cultures that use indirect communication, negotiators may have to infer preferences and priorities from changes—or the lack of them—in the other party's settlement proposal. In cross-cultural negotiations, the non-Westerner can understand the direct communications of the Westerner, but the Westerner has difficulty understanding the indirect communications of the non-Westerner.

An American manager who was leading a project to build an interface for a U.S. and Japanese customer-data system explained the problems her team was having this way: "In Japan, they want to talk and discuss. Then we take a break and they talk within the organization. They want to make sure that there's harmony in the rest of the organization. One of the hardest lessons for me was when I thought they were saying yes but they just meant 'I'm listening to you.'"

Idea in Practice

Four Barriers

The following cultural differences can cause destructive conflicts in a team:

- **Direct versus indirect communication.** Some team members use direct, explicit communication while others are indirect, for example, asking questions instead of pointing out problems with a project. When members see such differences as violations of their culture's communication norms, relationships can suffer.

- **Trouble with accents and fluency.** Members who aren't fluent in the team's dominant language may have difficulty communicating their knowledge. This can prevent the team from using their expertise and create frustration or perceptions of incompetence.

- **Differing attitudes toward hierarchy.** Team members from hierarchical cultures expect to be treated differently according to their status in the organization. Members from egalitarian cultures do not. Failure of some members to honor those expectations can cause humiliation or loss of stature and credibility.

- **Conflicting decision-making norms.** Members vary in how quickly they make decisions and in how much analysis they require beforehand. Someone who prefers making decisions quickly may grow frustrated with those who need more time.

Four Interventions

Your team's unique circumstances can help you determine how to respond to multicultural conflicts. Consider these options:

Intervention type	When to use	Example
Adaptation: working with or around differences	Members are willing to acknowledge cultural differences and figure out how to live with them.	An American engineer working on a team that included Israelis was shocked by their in-your-face, argumentative style. Once he noticed they confronted each other and not just him—and still worked well together—he realized confrontations weren't personal attacks and accepted their style.

Intervention type	When to use	Example
Structural intervention: reorganizing to reduce friction	The team has obvious subgroups, or members cling to negative stereotypes of one another.	An international research team's leader realized that when he led meetings, members "shut down" because they felt intimidated by his executive status. After he hired a consultant to run future meetings, members participated more.
Managerial intervention: making final decisions without team involvement	Rarely; for instance, a new team needs guidance in establishing productive norms.	A software development team's lingua franca was English, but some members spoke with pronounced accents. The manager explained they'd been chosen for their task expertise, not fluency in English. And she directed them to tell customers: "I realize I have an accent. If you don't understand what I'm saying, just stop me and ask questions."
Exit: voluntary or involuntary removal of a team member	Emotions are running high, and too much face has been lost on both sides to salvage the situation.	When two members of a multicultural consulting team couldn't resolve their disagreement over how to approach problems, one member left the firm.

The differences between direct and indirect communication can cause serious damage to relationships when team projects run into problems. When the American manager quoted above discovered that several flaws in the system would significantly disrupt company operations, she pointed this out in an e-mail to her American boss and the Japanese team members. Her boss appreciated the direct warnings; her Japanese colleagues were embarrassed, because she had violated their norms for uncovering and discussing problems. Their reaction was to provide her with less access to the people and information she needed to monitor progress. They would probably have responded better if she had pointed out the problems indirectly—for example, by asking them what would happen if a certain part of the system was not functioning properly, even though she knew full well that it was malfunctioning and also what the implications were.

As our research indicates is so often true, communication challenges create barriers to effective teamwork by reducing information sharing, creating interpersonal conflict, or both. In Japan, a typical response to direct confrontation is to isolate the norm violator. This American manager was isolated not just socially but also physically. She told us, "They literally put my office in a storage room, where I had desks stacked from floor to ceiling and I was the only person there. So they totally isolated me, which was a pretty loud signal to me that I was not a part of the inside circle and that they would communicate with me only as needed."

Her direct approach had been intended to solve a problem, and in one sense, it did, because her project was launched problem-free. But her norm violations exacerbated the challenges of working with her Japanese colleagues and limited her ability to uncover any other problems that might have derailed the project later on.

Trouble with accents and fluency

Although the language of international business is English, misunderstandings or deep frustration may occur because of nonnative speakers' accents, lack of fluency, or problems with translation or usage. These may also influence perceptions of status or competence.

For example, a Latin American member of a multicultural consulting team lamented, "Many times I felt that because of the language difference, I didn't have the words to say some things that I was thinking. I noticed that when I went to these interviews with the U.S. guy, he would tend to lead the interviews, which was understandable but also disappointing, because we are at the same level. I had very good questions, but he would take the lead."

When we interviewed an American member of a U.S.-Japanese team that was assessing the potential expansion of a U.S. retail chain into Japan, she described one American teammate this way: "He was not interested in the Japanese consultants' feedback and felt that because they weren't as fluent as he was, they weren't intelligent enough and, therefore, could add no value." The team member described was responsible for assessing one aspect of the feasibility of expansion into Japan. Without input from the Japanese experts, he risked overestimating opportunities and underestimating challenges.

Nonfluent team members may well be the most expert on the team, but their difficulty communicating knowledge makes it hard for the team to recognize and utilize their expertise. If teammates become frustrated or impatient with a lack of fluency, interpersonal conflicts can arise. Nonnative speakers may become less motivated to contribute, or anxious about their performance evaluations and future career prospects. The organization as a whole pays a greater price: Its investment in a multicultural team fails to pay off.

Some teams, we learned, use language differences to resolve (rather than create) tensions. A team of U.S. and Latin American buyers was negotiating with a team from a Korean supplier. The negotiations took place in Korea, but the discussions were conducted in English. Frequently the Koreans would caucus at the table by speaking Korean. The buyers, frustrated, would respond by appearing to caucus in Spanish—though they discussed only inconsequential current events and sports, in case any of the Koreans spoke Spanish. Members of the team who didn't speak Spanish pretended to participate, to the great amusement of their teammates. This approach proved effective: It conveyed to the Koreans in an appropriately indirect way that their caucuses in Korean were frustrating and annoying to the other side. As a result, both teams cut back on sidebar conversations.

Differing attitudes toward hierarchy and authority

A challenge inherent in multicultural teamwork is that by design, teams have a rather flat structure. But team members from some cultures, in which people are treated differently according to their status in an organization, are uncomfortable on flat teams. If they defer to higher-status team members, their behavior will be seen as appropriate when most of the team comes from a hierarchical culture; but they may damage their stature and credibility—and even face humiliation—if most of the team comes from an egalitarian culture.

One manager of Mexican heritage, who was working on a credit and underwriting team for a bank, told us, "In Mexican culture, you're always supposed to be humble. So whether you understand something or not, you're supposed to put it in the form of a question. You have to keep it open-ended, out of respect. I think that actually worked against me, because the Americans thought I really didn't know what I was talking about. So it made me feel like they thought I was wavering on my answer."

When, as a result of differing cultural norms, team members believe they've been treated disrespectfully, the whole project can blow up. In another Korean-U.S. negotiation, the American members of a due diligence team were having difficulty getting information from their Korean counterparts, so they complained directly to higher-level Korean management, nearly wrecking the deal. The higher-level managers were offended because hierarchy is strictly adhered to in Korean organizations and culture. It should have been their own lower-level people, not the U.S. team members, who came to them with a problem. And the Korean team members were mortified that their bosses had been involved before they themselves could brief them. The crisis was resolved only when high-level U.S. managers made a trip to Korea, conveying appropriate respect for their Korean counterparts.

Conflicting norms for decision making

Cultures differ enormously when it comes to decision making—particularly, how quickly decisions should be made and how much analysis is required beforehand. Not surprisingly, U.S. managers like to make decisions very quickly and with relatively little analysis by comparison with managers from other countries.

A Brazilian manager at an American company who was negotiating to buy Korean products destined for Latin America told us, "On the first day, we agreed on three points, and on the second day, the U.S.-Spanish side wanted to start with point four. But the Korean side wanted to go back and rediscuss points one through three. My boss almost had an attack."

What U.S. team members learn from an experience like this is that the American way simply cannot be imposed on other cultures. Managers from other cultures may, for example, decline to share information until they understand the full scope of a project. But they have learned that they can't simply ignore the desire of their American counterparts to make decisions quickly. What to do? The best solution seems to be to make minor concessions on process— to learn to adjust to and even respect another approach to decision making. For example, American managers have learned to keep their impatient bosses away from team meetings and give them frequent if brief updates. A comparable lesson for managers from other cultures is to be explicit about what they need—saying, for example, "We have to see the big picture before we talk details."

Four Strategies

The most successful teams and managers we interviewed used four strategies for dealing with these challenges: adaptation (acknowledging cultural gaps openly and working around them), structural intervention (changing the shape of the team), managerial intervention (setting norms early or bringing in a higher-level manager), and exit (removing a team member when other options have failed). There is no one right way to deal with a particular kind of multicultural problem; identifying the type of challenge is only the first step. The more crucial step is assessing the circumstances—or "enabling situational conditions"—under which the team is working. For example, does the project allow any flexibility for change, or do deadlines make that impossible? Are there additional resources available that might be tapped? Is the team permanent or temporary? Does the team's manager have the autonomy to make a decision about changing the team in some way? Once the situational conditions have been analyzed, the team's leader can identify an appropriate response (see the table "Identifying the right strategy").

Identifying the right strategy

The most successful teams and managers we interviewed use four strategies for dealing with problems: adaptation (acknowledging cultural gaps openly and working around them), structural intervention (changing the shape of the team), managerial intervention (setting norms early or bringing in a higher-level manager), and exit (removing a team member when other options have failed). Adaptation is the ideal strategy because the team works effectively to solve its own problem with minimal input from management—and, most important, learns from the experience. The guide below can help you identify the right strategy once you have identified both the problem and the "enabling situational conditions" that apply to the team.

Representative problems	Enabling situational conditions	Strategy	Complicating factors
• Conflict arises from decision-making differences • Misunderstanding or stonewalling arises from communication differences	• Team members can attribute a challenge to culture rather than personality • Higher-level managers are not available or the team would be embarrassed to involve them	**Adaptation**	• Team members must be exceptionally aware • Negotiating a common understanding takes time
• The team is affected by emotional tensions relating to fluency issues or prejudice • Team members are inhibited by perceived status differences among teammates	• The team can be subdivided to mix cultures or expertise • Tasks can be subdivided	**Structural intervention**	• If team members aren't carefully distributed, subgroups can strengthen preexisting differences • Subgroup solutions have to fit back together

Representative problems	Enabling situational conditions	Strategy	Complicating factors
• Violations of hierarchy have resulted in loss of face • An absence of ground rules is causing conflict	• The problem has produced a high level of emotion • The team has reached a stalemate • A higher-level manager is able and willing to intervene	**Managerial intervention**	• The team becomes overly dependent on the manager • Team members may be sidelined or resistant
• A team member cannot adjust to the challenge at hand and has become unable to contribute to the project	• The team is permanent rather than temporary • Emotions are beyond the point of intervention • Too much face has been lost	**Exit**	• Talent and training costs are lost

Adaptation

Some teams find ways to work with or around the challenges they face, adapting practices or attitudes without making changes to the group's membership or assignments. Adaptation works when team members are willing to acknowledge and name their cultural differences and to assume responsibility for figuring out how to live with them. It's often the best possible approach to a problem, because it typically involves less managerial time than other strategies; and because team members participate in solving the problem themselves, they learn from the process. When team members have this mind-set, they can be creative about protecting their own substantive differences while acceding to the processes of others.

An American software engineer located in Ireland who was working with an Israeli account management team from his own company told us how shocked he was by the Israelis' in-your-face style: "There were definitely different ways of approaching issues and discussing them. There is something pretty common to the Israeli culture: They like to argue. I tend to try to collaborate more, and it got very stressful for me until I figured out how to kind of merge the cultures."

The software engineer adapted. He imposed some structure on the Israelis that helped him maintain his own style of being thoroughly prepared; that accommodation enabled him to accept the Israeli style. He also noticed that team members weren't just confronting him; they confronted one another but were able to work together effectively nevertheless. He realized that the confrontation was not personal but cultural.

In another example, an American member of a postmerger consulting team was frustrated by the hierarchy of the French company his team was working with. He felt that a meeting with certain French managers who were not directly involved in the merger "wouldn't deliver any value to me or for purposes of the project," but said that he had come to understand that "it was very important to really involve all the people there" if the integration was ultimately to work.

A U.S. and UK multicultural team tried to use their differing approaches to decision making to reach a higher-quality decision. This approach, called fusion, is getting serious attention from political scientists and from government officials dealing with multicultural populations that want to protect their cultures rather than integrate or assimilate. If the team had relied exclusively on the Americans' "forge ahead" approach, it might not have recognized the pitfalls that lay ahead and might later have had to back up and start over. Meanwhile, the UK members would have been gritting their teeth and saying "We told you things were moving too fast." If the team had used the "Let's think about this" UK approach, it might have wasted a lot of time trying to identify every pitfall, including the most unlikely, while the U.S. members chomped at the bit and muttered about analysis paralysis. The strength of this team was that some of its members were willing to forge ahead and some were willing to work through pitfalls. To accommodate them all, the team did both—moving not quite as fast as the U.S. members would have on their own and not quite as thoroughly as the UK members would have.

Structural intervention

A structural intervention is a deliberate reorganization or reassignment designed to reduce interpersonal friction or to remove a source of conflict for one or more groups. This approach can be extremely effective when obvious subgroups demarcate the team (for example, headquarters versus national subsidiaries) or if team members are proud, defensive, threatened, or clinging to negative stereotypes of one another.

A member of an investment research team scattered across continental Europe, the UK, and the U.S. described for us how his manager resolved conflicts stemming from status differences and language tensions among the team's three "tribes." The manager started by having the team meet face-to-face twice a year, not to discuss mundane day-to-day problems (of which there were many) but to identify a set of values that the team would use to direct and evaluate its progress. At the first meeting, he realized that when he started to speak, everyone else "shut down," waiting to hear what he had to say. So he hired a consultant to run future meetings. The consultant didn't represent a hierarchical threat and was therefore able to get lots of participation from team members.

Another structural intervention might be to create smaller working groups of mixed cultures or mixed corporate identities in order to get at information that is not forthcoming from the team as a whole. The manager of the team that was evaluating retail opportunities in Japan used this approach. When she realized that the female Japanese consultants would not participate if the group got large, or if their male superior was present, she broke the team up into smaller groups to try to solve problems. She used this technique repeatedly and made a point of changing the subgroups' membership each time so that team members got to know and respect everyone else on the team.

The subgrouping technique involves risks, however. It buffers people who are not working well together or not participating in the larger group for one reason or another. Sooner or later the team will have to assemble the pieces that the subgroups have come up with, so this approach relies on another structural intervention: Someone must become a mediator in order to see that the various pieces fit together.

Managerial intervention

When a manager behaves like an arbitrator or a judge, making a final decision without team involvement, neither the manager nor the team gains much insight into why the team has stalemated. But it is possible for team members to use managerial intervention effectively to sort out problems.

When an American refinery-safety expert with significant experience throughout East Asia got stymied during a project in China, she called in her company's higher-level managers in Beijing to talk to the higher-level managers to whom the Chinese refinery's managers reported. Unlike the Western team members who breached etiquette by approaching the superiors of their Korean counterparts, the safety expert made sure to respect hierarchies in both organizations.

"Trying to resolve the issues," she told us, "the local management at the Chinese refinery would end up having conferences with our Beijing office and also with the upper management within the refinery. Eventually they understood that we weren't trying to insult them or their culture or to tell them they were bad in any way. We were trying to help. They eventually understood that there were significant fire and safety issues. But we actually had to go up some levels of management to get those resolved."

Managerial intervention to set norms early in a team's life can really help the team start out with effective processes. In one instance reported to us, a multicultural software development team's lingua franca was English, but some members, though they spoke grammatically correct English, had a very pronounced accent. In setting the ground rules for the team, the manager addressed the challenge directly, telling the members that they had been chosen for their task expertise, not their fluency in English, and that the team was going to have to work around language problems. As the project moved to the customer-services training stage, the manager advised the team members to acknowledge their accents up front.

She said they should tell customers, "I realize I have an accent. If you don't understand what I'm saying, just stop me and ask questions."

Exit

Possibly because many of the teams we studied were project based, we found that leaving the team was an infrequent strategy for managing challenges. In short-term situations, unhappy team members often just waited out the project. When teams were permanent, producing products or services, the exit of one or more members was a strategy of last resort, but it was used—either voluntarily or after a formal request from management. Exit was likely when emotions were running high and too much face had been lost on both sides to salvage the situation.

An American member of a multicultural consulting team described the conflict between two senior consultants, one a Greek woman and the other a Polish man, over how to approach problems: "The woman from Greece would say, 'Here's the way I think we should do it.' It would be something that she was in control of. The guy from Poland would say, 'I think we should actually do it this way instead.' The woman would kind of turn red in the face, upset, and say, 'I just don't think that's the right way of doing it.' It would definitely switch from just professional differences to personal differences.

"The woman from Greece ended up leaving the firm. That was a direct result of probably all the different issues going on between these people. It really just wasn't a good fit. I've found that oftentimes when you're in consulting, you have to adapt to the culture, obviously, but you have to adapt just as much to the style of whoever is leading the project."

Though multicultural teams face challenges that are not directly attributable to cultural differences, such differences underlay whatever problem needed to be addressed in many of the teams we studied. Furthermore, while serious in their own right when they have a negative effect on team functioning, cultural challenges may also unmask fundamental managerial problems. Managers who intervene early and set norms; teams and managers who structure social interaction and work to engage everyone on the team; and teams that can see problems as stemming from culture, not personality, approach challenges with good humor and creativity. Managers who have to intervene when the team has reached a stalemate may be able to get the team moving again, but they seldom empower it to help itself the next time a stalemate occurs.

When frustrated team members take some time to think through challenges and possible solutions themselves, it can make a huge difference. Take, for example, this story about a financial-services call center. The members of the call-center team were all fluent Spanish-speakers, but some were North Americans and some were Latin Americans. Team performance, measured by calls answered per hour, was lagging. One Latin American was taking twice as long with her calls as the rest of the team. She was handling callers' questions appropriately, but she was also engaging in chitchat. When her teammates confronted her for being a free rider (they resented having to make up for her low call rate), she immediately acknowledged the problem, admitting that she did not know how to end the call politely—chitchat being normal in her culture. They rallied to help her: Using their technology, they would break into any of her calls that went overtime, excusing themselves to the customer, offering to take over the call, and saying that this employee was urgently needed to help out on a different call. The team's solution worked in the short run, and the employee got better at ending her calls in the long run.

In another case, the Indian manager of a multicultural team coordinating a companywide IT project found himself frustrated when he and a teammate from Singapore met with two Japanese members of the coordinating team to try to get the Japan section to deliver its part of the project. The Japanese members seemed to be saying yes, but in the Indian manager's view, their follow-through was insufficient. He considered and rejected the idea of going up the hierarchy to the Japanese team members' boss, and decided instead to try to build consensus with the whole Japanese IT team, not just the two members on the coordinating team. He and his Singapore teammate put together an eBusiness road show, took it to Japan, invited the whole IT team to view it at a lunch meeting, and walked through success stories about other parts of the organization that had aligned with the company's larger business priorities. It was rather subtle, he told us, but it worked. The Japanese IT team wanted to be spotlighted in future eBusiness road shows. In the end, the whole team worked well together—and no higher-level manager had to get involved.

Originally published in November 2006. Reprint R0611D

L'Oréal Masters Multiculturalism

by Hae-Jung Hong and Yves L. Doz

AT THE HEART OF EVERY global business lies a tension that is never fully resolved: Achieving economies of scale and scope demands some uniformity and integration of activities across markets. However, serving regional and national markets requires the adaptation of products, services, and business models to local conditions. As U.S. and European companies increasingly look for customers in emerging economies, both the advantages of global scale and the need for local differentiation will only increase.

It's easy to get the balance wrong. Some offerings may feel like commodities—think refrigerators and washing machines—yet there are often important variations in the way people use them. An Italian washing machine, for instance, has to be made to rather different specs than a Swedish one. Others, such as restaurants and cafés, come across as intrinsically local, yet global formulas and brands do succeed—think Benihana, Wagamama, and Starbucks.

The tension between global integration and local responsiveness is especially high when product development and marketing require complex knowledge. This kind of knowledge—usually tacit and collective, revealed only in action and interaction—is often the mainspring of a company's competitive advantage. The trouble is that tacit knowledge functions best within national boundaries, where workers share a language and cultural and institutional norms and can draw on strong interpersonal networks. Without close, face-to-face interaction between knowledge creators and users, an understanding of how bits of information fit together may be lost and the knowledge may become unusable. Further, when tacit knowledge must cross borders, it is often reduced to information that moves easily (words and numbers, for instance) but may then fall prey to local misinterpretations that are difficult to detect from afar.

The French cosmetics giant L'Oréal exemplifies this global-local tension. It has built a portfolio of brands from many cultures— French, of course (L'Oréal Paris, Garnier, Lancôme), but also American (Maybelline, Kiehl's, SoftSheen-Carson), British (The Body Shop), Italian (Giorgio Armani), and Japanese (Shu Uemura). The company now has offices in more than 130 countries, and in 2012 over half its sales came from new markets outside Europe and North America, mostly in emerging economies, up from only a third as recently as 2009.

In 2012, sales grew in the Asia Pacific region by 18.4% and in Africa and the Middle East by 17.6%, without significant acquisitions. Despite the financial crises in Europe and North America, L'Oréal has been growing and gaining market share, mostly at the expense of its competitors. It is the uncontested world leader in skin care, makeup, and hair color and a close second to P&G in hair care worldwide. Since 2004 L'Oréal's revenue has increased by half and its profits have almost doubled, with an increase in net profits of 17.6% in 2012 alone.

Yet this remarkable global success was built largely by a management team strongly rooted in its home culture. Traditionally employees became part of management over many years, weaving a dense network of relationships through which knowledge about products, cultures, and how to work together was internalized. Since its inception, more than a century ago, L'Oréal has had only five CEOs (including the founder), all but one with long tenures and all promoted from within. Only a few foreigners have become senior executives. Lindsay Owen-Jones, who was CEO from 1988 to 2006, was one of them. Although an Englishman, he was described

Idea in Brief

As the cosmetics company L'Oréal has transformed itself from a very French business into a global leader, it has grappled with the tension that's at the heart of every global enterprise: Achieving economies of scale and scope requires some uniformity and integration of activities across markets. However, serving regional and national markets requires the adaptation of products, services, and business models to local conditions. Since the late 1990s, the L'Oréal Paris brand—which accounts for half the sales of the consumer products division—has dealt with that tension by nurturing a pool of managers with mixed cultural backgrounds, placing them at the center of knowledge-based interactions in the company's most critical activity: new-product development. L'Oréal Paris builds product development teams around these managers, who, by virtue of their upbringing and experiences, have gained familiarity with the norms and behaviors of multiple cultures and can switch easily among them. They are uniquely qualified to play several crucial roles: spotting new-product opportunities, facilitating communication across cultural boundaries, assimilating newcomers, and serving as a cultural buffer between executives and their direct reports and between subsidiaries and headquarters.

by members of L'Oréal's founding family as *Français dans l'âme* ("French in his soul"). For decades, L'Oréal recruited few senior executives from outside. After several years the exceptions took pains to explain that they had worked for L'Oréal for a long time and prided themselves on their perfect French.

As its global-local tensions have mounted, L'Oréal has managed them by deploying professionals with multicultural backgrounds in new-product development, the company's most critical source of competitive advantage. That strategy, according to top management, is the main reason for L'Oréal's impressive success in emerging markets. As the company has transformed itself from a very French beauty products business to a global leader, multicultural executives have come to play a critical role in product development not just in Paris but also in New York, Tokyo, Shanghai, Rio, and Mumbai.

Achieving Global-Local Balance

L'Oréal's main consumer-products categories are all highly sensitive to global economies of scale and scope, yet to win customers they must also be responsive to local preferences. This tension is perhaps most critical in the L'Oréal Paris brand, which is sold in mass markets worldwide and accounts for half the sales of the consumer products division.

L'Oréal also has to maintain a steady stream of new products (every year, roughly 20% are new) in order to extend market share in the face of stiff competition from rivals such as Estée Lauder and Revlon and units of global giants such as Unilever and P&G. L'Oréal, which invests 3.5% of its revenue in R&D, outspends all its major competitors: Revlon, for instance, spends 1.7% on R&D, and Estée Lauder about 1%.

As L'Oréal managers confront those challenges, they must be mindful that their products are much more than chemical mixes. They are global symbols of fashion and sophistication, appealing to the idealized self-image of customers. Technical innovation and responsiveness to local tastes must not undermine the brand.

Traditional approaches to internationalization probably would not have resolved L'Oréal's global-local tensions. Structural solutions, such as setting up largely autonomous subsidiaries and regional entities (which might have compromised economies of scale) or global business units (which might have ignored the richness of cultural differences across markets), would not have worked for most L'Oréal products, given their need for both local responsiveness and global integration. Refocusing the company on either a more local or a more global portfolio would have been tantamount to letting the tail wag the dog, forfeiting L'Oréal's many marketing and distribution advantages.

The only alternative to internationalizing the structure was to internationalize the management team. That is what L'Oréal did, but with a twist. The rapid infusion of foreign executives would have disrupted the tightly knit community of senior managers so critical to L'Oréal's success. Relying on global teams—whether function- or project-based—would have been equally difficult. Culturally diverse teams often experience the so-called Tower of Babel syndrome: Their members talk past one another, and teamwork breaks down. Companies quickly realize that little knowledge is actually shared; even seemingly universal and explicit knowledge, such as mathematics, is open to interpretation.

L'Oréal has dealt with these shortcomings by recruiting and building teams around individual managers, who by virtue of their upbringing and experience have gained familiarity with the norms and behaviors of multiple cultures and can switch easily among them.

International Talent

Since the late 1990s, when L'Oréal started to recruit internationally for positions at headquarters, L'Oréal Paris—the unit where we conducted our research—has placed executives from mixed cultural backgrounds in its most critical activity: new-product development. These managers account for a small proportion of L'Oréal Paris employees but for more than a third of the unit's product development team managers—a balance the unit has maintained for more than 10 years.

L'Oréal Paris generally has about 40 product development teams, each working on a different concept. A team consists of three or four people, two of whom may be multicultural. For example, in a team we spoke with that is working on women's hair-care products for Latin America, a Lebanese-Spanish-American manager was in charge of hair color while a French-Irish-Cambodian was in charge of hair care. They shared an office so that they could exchange ideas.

Developing a new product takes at least a year of knowledge exchanges among the product development team, regional subsidiaries, and functional units in France, such as R&D. In addition to interacting with their peers, who may come from different cultures, team managers must discuss their work with top management, formally and informally, as it progresses.

Once a new-product concept is ready, the team presents it at Réunion Internationale, the consumer products division's annual event, held at the Paris headquarters. The teams pitch their launch action plans to regional directors from around the globe, who come looking for ideas that might be ready to hit the market in one or two years.

The multicultural managers are drawn from three pools. The most seasoned come from the company's international subsidiaries and have at least five years of experience in sales and marketing. A few are recruited from other global companies. The third and youngest group consists of graduates of leading international business schools. The recruits undergo a 12-month training program in Paris, New York, Singapore, or Rio, followed by management development programs at Cedep, an executive education consortium in France.

After spending two or three years in global product development at headquarters, the more experienced managers usually return to their home regions as directors, responsible for managing a brand or function. Most of those recruited from business schools remain for another few years in product development at headquarters. After this second tour they, too, usually go to a regional office at the director level, though some remain in Paris. Their promotion prospects, like those of all employees, depend on performance.

An increasing number of multiculturals are starting to find their way into senior management in the company—a sign of the success of the approach. Among the people we met, one Hong Kong–British–French project manager (recruited at headquarters) was subsequently promoted to lead the team developing all facial products for the East Asian market, and an Indian-American-French project manager (recruited from the Indian subsidiary) moved to another division with a significant promotion.

In sum—and there is an important message here for other multinational companies—L'Oréal nurtures a pool of multicultural managers, placing them at the center of knowledge-based interactions among brands, regions, and functions. Let's look at what these young men and women offer the company in return.

The Advantages of Multiculturals

A person rooted in more than one culture is usually able to spot and reconcile differences in understanding and communication, serving as a buffer both within teams and more broadly in the organization. In addition, he or she will probably be more open to adapting to multiple mind-sets and communication modes; it's well known that people find it easier to learn new languages if they have grown up speaking more than one. These skills equip L'Oréal's multiculturals to play five critical roles.

Recognizing new-product opportunities

L'Oréal Paris finds that multiculturals are better placed than others to draw analogies among cultural groups. According to a director who worked with multiculturals for five years, "Their background is a kind of master class in holding more than one idea at the same time. They think as if they were French, American, or Chinese, and all of these together at once."

This very flexible perspective can lead to unexpected opportunities for product innovation. For instance, a French-Irish-Cambodian manager working on skin care noticed that many tinted face creams in Asia had a lifting effect, which minimizes wrinkles. In Europe, creams tended to be either tinted (and considered as makeup) or lifting (and considered as skin care). Drawing on his knowledge of Asian beauty trends and their increasing popularity in Europe, he and his team developed a tinted cream with lifting effects for the French market, which proved to be a success.

Although people rooted in one culture can also uncover such opportunities, multiculturals are more likely to do so—and to do so faster—because they have been dealing with cultural complexities since childhood. As an Indian-American-French manager in a team that launched a men's skin care line in Southeast Asia explained, "I am able to do this because I have a stock of references in different languages: English, Hindi, and French. I read books in three different languages, meet people from different countries, eat food from different countries, and so on. I cannot think about things in one way."

Preventing losses in translation

Even when there's a common syntax or language, as in mathematical and chemical formulas, cross-cultural semantic differences can cause confusion. What the person initiating a communication means is not necessarily what the person receiving the communication hears. The problem thus shifts to who interprets what, and how accurately—a critical issue in the design of new products.

For instance, a French manager's product test failed because he asked a German colleague in the laboratory to translate the characterization of some hair features. Through conversations with an English-French-German manager, the French manager discovered that there had been a gap between what he meant and what the German heard. It was a nuanced difference: The words were the same, but their meaning was not. He had to run the test again, at significant cost. Since then, the multicultural manager who spotted the difference has been called on frequently to decode communications between headquarters and the German office.

Integrating outsiders

Teams staffed with people who are not multicultural find it hard to assimilate newcomers with different behaviors and modes of communication, particularly when the team has developed its own norms or its members belong predominantly to one culture. Given the intensity of a team's internal interactions, incumbent team members can quickly resort to stereotypes about a newcomer, and the situation can become toxic. The presence of a multicultural member can help prevent this dynamic from taking hold.

Consider the experience of a Hong Kong–British–French director: "After a new person joined my team from the Shanghai office, a member complained that she was 'very rude.' I said, 'Let's give her more time to adjust. Maybe she's not being rude and that's just how she expresses herself. Why don't you also try to adapt to her?' When I went to Shanghai, I had a meeting with my new team member and found she was not being rude. The way she expressed herself was direct, without bad intention. I didn't tell her about the complaints but gave some advice on how to better work with people whose cultures are different. When I returned to HQ, I told my group about my experience with the new member. Things became much better."

Emulating multicultural managers

Managers rooted in more than one culture have many skills that allow them to fill five crucial roles. Other managers can learn to play the first two roles through training and management development programs. But the final three roles are based on skills acquired through early life experiences and are therefore more difficult for others to learn. The careful management of international assignments can help. Be cautious about short-term rotations: Without deep exposure to national contexts, managers concentrate on what's common across cultures instead of what's different. As a result, their cultural sensitivity is dulled rather than sharpened.

Role	How multiculturals do it	How others can learn
1. Recognizing new-product opportunities	Sensitivity to one's own and others' cultures	Training with multiculturals and repatriates
	Cultural awareness and curiosity	One-on-one coaching by multiculturals
2. Preventing losses in translation	Cultural empathy	
	Multilingual skills	Regular evaluation by an HR specialist knowledgeable about multiculturals' competence and skills
3. Integrating outsiders	Contextual understanding and sensitivity	
4. Mediating with bosses	Semantic awareness	Foreign language and semantics training
5. Bridging differences between subsidiaries and headquarters	Ability to switch among cultural frames of reference and communication modes	Enhanced promotion prospects for foreign language speakers
		Opportunities to carry out leadership responsibilities in a foreign language

If a newcomer is disruptive because of personal style or personality, there may be little anyone can do. But if the issue originates in cultural differences, which it often does, multiculturals can help integrate the outsider. They can perform this function because they are adept at moving from one mode of interaction to another. They grew up doing so—switching from one parent to another, or from school to home.

Mediating with bosses

The role of cultural buffer is important at L'Oréal Paris, especially for reducing the potential for conflicts between the multicultural product-development teams and the people they report to, who are, for the most part, French. Here's how a multicultural manager explained one aspect of his role as team leader: "My French boss never starts meetings on time. So whenever we have a meeting planned with him, we can get frustrated if we are not flexible. If I am running behind myself, I make sure to tell my team members in advance why I am behind and ask them for their next availabilities. Conflicts may still exist in my team, but we handle them more tolerantly."

Bridging differences between subsidiaries and headquarters

Multicultural managers have frequently defused acrimonious communications between a subsidiary and L'Oréal Paris. For example, on a project to develop an organic shampoo for the European market, the product development team in Paris asked the Indian unit to find a rare local plant that would provide a key ingredient. The Indians told the team that they would "do their best" but sat on the request. As the team's Indian-American-French leader told us, "Eventually the Indian manager said, 'We need confirmation that this ingredient can really please consumers.'"

At this point, the team leader understood that the initial "We'll do our best" (which the French interpreted as a clear yes) was actually a polite way of saying that they wouldn't do anything. The "We need confirmation" follow-up signaled that the request was too difficult—but the Indians did not want to come out and say that and thus fail to honor a commitment. The leader realized that if he told headquarters that India wouldn't come up with the goods, he risked triggering open conflict between the two parties. Instead, he worked with both to explore other ingredients that would not be so challenging to source.

The team leader grasped that there had not yet been enough collaboration or social interaction between the two teams to allow them to decode each other's expressions of expectations. He could also see that this particular misunderstanding might undermine trust and make more-important tasks harder. (Ultimately he found a substitute ingredient and dropped the matter.) This manager could play a bridging role because he had deep knowledge about both Indian and French ways of expressing commitment, strong communication skills, intense cultural sensitivity, and high flexibility—a bundle of qualities seldom found among managers rooted in just one culture. For a global company to deploy multiculturals strategically, HR should appoint a manager to lead a program for developing and nurturing them. This manager should obviously be knowledgeable about the competence and skills of these individuals and how they differ from those of other employees. Because of considerable variation among multiculturals themselves, the manager needs to tailor a training system to each one. With this support, commitment to the program from top managers, and the granting of some autonomy in their work, multicultural managers can make a huge difference in whether a company is able to balance global and local imperatives by learning from cultural differences—or instead suffers from them.

As markets and competencies have become more dispersed and differentiated with the strategic thrust into emerging regions, companies need to reverse the old knowledge flows (from their home country to far-flung subsidiaries) and instead learn how to learn from their peripheries. Culturally this is difficult. It calls for a shift from an ethnocentric approach to a truly global network. L'Oréal's strategic use of multicultural managers provides a shortcut: These managers can integrate knowledge from many locations to develop successful new products and minimize conflict between home-country and international executives. It's an approach that can transfer easily to other industry and functional contexts in which complex knowledge from multiple cultures must be coordinated and shared.

Originally published in June 2013. Reprint R1306J

Making Differences Matter

A New Paradigm for Managing Diversity. **by David A. Thomas and Robin J. Ely**

WHY SHOULD COMPANIES CONCERN THEMSELVES with diversity? Until recently, many managers answered this question with the assertion that discrimination is wrong, both legally and morally. But today managers are voicing a second notion as well. A more diverse workforce, they say, will increase organizational effectiveness. It will lift morale, bring greater access to new segments of the marketplace, and enhance productivity. In short, they claim, diversity will be good for business.

Yet if this is true—and we believe it is—where are the positive impacts of diversity? Numerous and varied initiatives to increase diversity in corporate America have been under way for more than two decades. Rarely, however, have those efforts spurred leaps in organizational effectiveness. Instead, many attempts to increase diversity in the workplace have backfired, sometimes even heightening tensions among employees and hindering a company's performance.

This article offers an explanation for why diversity efforts are not fulfilling their promise and presents a new paradigm for understanding—and leveraging—diversity. It is our belief that there is a distinct way to unleash the powerful benefits of a diverse workforce. Although these benefits include increased profitability, they go beyond financial measures to encompass learning, creativity, flexibility, organizational and individual growth, and the ability of a company to adjust rapidly and successfully to market changes. The desired transformation, however, requires a fundamental change in the attitudes and behaviors of an organization's leadership. And that will come only when senior managers abandon an underlying and flawed assumption about diversity and replace it with a broader understanding.

Most people assume that workplace diversity is about increasing racial, national, gender, or class representation—in other words, recruiting and retaining more people from traditionally underrepresented "identity groups." Taking this commonly held assumption as a starting point, we set out six years ago to investigate its link to organizational effectiveness. We soon found that thinking of diversity simply in terms of identity-group representation inhibited effectiveness.

Organizations usually take one of two paths in managing diversity. In the name of equality and fairness, they encourage (and expect) women and people of color to blend in. Or they set them apart in jobs that relate specifically to their backgrounds, assigning them, for example, to areas that require them to interface with clients or customers of the same identity group. African American M.B.A.'s often find themselves marketing products to inner-city communities; Hispanics frequently market to Hispanics or work for Latin American subsidiaries. In those kinds of cases, companies are operating on the assumption that the main virtue identity groups have to offer is a knowledge of their own people. This assumption is limited—and limiting—and detrimental to diversity efforts.

What we suggest here is that diversity goes beyond increasing the number of different identity-group affiliations on the payroll to recognizing that such an effort is merely the first step in managing a diverse workforce for the organization's utmost benefit. Diversity should be understood as *the varied perspectives and approaches to work* that members of different identity groups bring.

Idea in Brief

You know that workforce diversity is smart business: It opens markets, lifts morale, and enhances productivity. So why do most diversity initiatives backfire—heightening tensions and *hindering* corporate performance?

Many of us simply hire employees with diverse backgrounds—then await the payoff. We don't enable employees' differences to transform *how our organization does work.*

When employees use their differences to shape new goals, pro-cesses, leadership approaches, and teams, they bring more of themselves to work. They feel more committed to their jobs—and their companies grow.

How to activate this virtuous cycle? Transcend two existing diversity paradigms: **assimilation** ("we're all the same") or **differentiation** ("we celebrate differences"). Adopt a new paradigm—**integration**—that enables employees' differences to matter.

Women, Hispanics, Asian Americans, African Americans, Native Americans—these groups and others outside the mainstream of corporate America don't bring with them just their "insider information." They bring different, important, and competitively relevant knowledge and perspectives about how to actually *do work*—how to design processes, reach goals, frame tasks, create effective teams, communicate ideas, and lead. When allowed to, members of these groups can help companies grow and improve by challenging basic assumptions about an organization's functions, strategies, operations, practices, and procedures. And in doing so, they are able to bring more of their whole selves to the workplace and identify more fully with the work they do, setting in motion a virtuous circle. Certainly, indivivduals can be expected to contribute to a company their firsthand familiarity with niche markets. But only when companies start thinking about diversity more holistically—as providing fresh and meaningful approaches to work—and stop assuming that diversity relates simply to how a person looks or where he or she comes from, will they be able to reap its full rewards.

Two perspectives have guided most diversity initiatives to date: the *discrimination-and-fairness paradigm* and the *access-and-legitimacy paradigm*. But we have identified a new, emerging

Idea in Practice

	Assimilation paradigm	Differentiation paradigm
Premise	"We're all the same."	"We celebrate differences."
Strategy	Hire diverse employees; encourage uniform behavior.	Match diverse employees to niche markets.
Advantage	Promotes fair hiring.	Expands markets.
Disadvantages	Subverting differences to encourage harmony, companies miss out on new ideas. Feeling detached from their work, employees' underperform.	Pigeonholed, staff can't influence mainstream work. Employees feel exploited and excluded from other opportunities.
Example	At a consulting company emphasizing quantitative analysis, minority managers encounter skepticism when they suggest interviewing clients. Labeling the incident as racial discord, the firm doesn't explore the potentially valuable new consulting approach.	To improve oversees operations, a U.S. bank assigns Europeans to its foreign offices. They excel—but the company doesn't know why. Not integrating diversity into its culture and practices, it becomes vulnerable: "If the French team resigns, what will we do?!"

approach to this complex management issue. This approach, which we call the *learning-and-effectiveness paradigm,* incorporates aspects of the first two paradigms but goes beyond them by concretely connecting diversity to approaches to work. Our goal is to help business leaders see what their own approach to diversity currently is and how it may already have influenced their companies' diversity efforts. Managers can learn to assess whether they need to

The Integration Paradigm

The **integration paradigm** *transcends* assimilation and differentiation—promoting equal opportunity *and* valuing cultural differences. Result? Employees' diverse perspectives positively impact companies' work.

> *Example*: A public-interest law firm's all-white staff's clients are exclusively white. It hires female attorneys of color, who encourage it to pursue litigation challenging English-only policies. Since such cases didn't fall under traditional affirmative-action work, the firm had ignored them. By taking them, it begins serving more women—immigrants—and enhances the quality of its work. The attorneys of color feel valued, and the firm attracts competent, diverse staff.

Additional suggestions for achieving integration:

1. **Encourage open discussion of cultural backgrounds.**

> *Example*: A food company's Chinese chemist draws on her cooking—not her scientific—experience to solve a soup-flavoring problem. But to fit in, she avoids sharing the real source of her inspiration with her colleagues—all white men. Open discussion of cultural differences would engage her more fully in work and workplace relationships.

2. **Eliminate all forms of dominance (by hierarchy, function, race, gender, etc.) that inhibit full contribution.** When one firm opened its annual strategy conference to people from all hierarchy levels, everyone knew their contributions were valued.

3. **Secure organizational trust.** In diverse workforces, people share more feelings and ideas. Tensions naturally arise. Demonstrate your commitment to diversity by acknowledging tensions—and resolving them swiftly.

change their diversity initiatives and, if so, how to accomplish that change.

The following discussion will also cite several examples of how connecting the new definition of diversity to the actual *doing* of work has led some organizations to markedly better performance. The organizations differ in many ways—none are in the same industry, for instance—but they are united by one similarity: Their leaders realize that increasing demographic variation does not in itself increase organizational effectiveness. They realize that it is *how* a company defines diversity—and *what it does* with the experiences of being a diverse organization—that delivers on the promise.

The Discrimination-and-Fairness Paradigm

Using the discrimination-and-fairness paradigm is perhaps thus far the dominant way of understanding diversity. Leaders who look at diversity through this lens usually focus on equal opportunity, fair treatment, recruitment, and compliance with federal Equal Employment Opportunity requirements. The paradigm's underlying logic can be expressed as follows:

> Prejudice has kept members of certain demographic groups out of organizations such as ours. As a matter of fairness and to comply with federal mandates, we need to work toward restructuring the makeup of our organization to let it more closely reflect that of society. We need managerial processes that ensure that all our employees are treated equally and with respect and that some are not given unfair advantage over others.

Although it resembles the thinking behind traditional affirmative-action efforts, the discrimination-and-fairness paradigm does go beyond a simple concern with numbers. Companies that operate with this philosophical orientation often institute mentoring and career-development programs specifically for the women and people of color in their ranks and train other employees to respect cultural differences. Under this paradigm, nevertheless, progress in diversity is measured by how well the company achieves its recruitment and retention goals rather than by the degree to which conditions in the company allow employees to draw on their personal assets and perspectives to do their work more effectively. The staff, one might say, gets diversified, but the work does not.

What are some of the common characteristics of companies that have used the discrimination-and-fairness paradigm successfully to increase their demographic diversity? Our research indicates that they are usually run by leaders who value due process and equal treatment of all employees and who have the authority to use top-down directives to enforce initiatives based on those attitudes. Such companies are often bureaucratic in structure, with control processes in place for monitoring, measuring, and rewarding individual performance. And finally, they are often organizations with entrenched, easily observable cultures, in which values like fairness are widespread and deeply inculcated and codes of conduct are clear and unambiguous. (Perhaps the most extreme example of an organization in which all these factors are at work is the United States Army.)

Without doubt, there are benefits to this paradigm: it does tend to increase demographic diversity in an organization, and it often succeeds in promoting fair treatment. But it also has significant limitations. The first of these is that its color-blind, gender-blind ideal is to some degree built on the implicit assumption that "we are all the same" or "we aspire to being all the same." Under this paradigm, it is not desirable for diversification of the workforce to influence the organization's work or culture. The company should operate as if every person were of the same race, gender, and nationality. It is unlikely that leaders who manage diversity under this paradigm will explore how people's differences generate a potential diversity of effective ways of working, leading, viewing the market, managing people, and learning.

Not only does the discrimination-and-fairness paradigm insist that everyone is the same, but, with its emphasis on equal treatment, it puts pressure on employees to make sure that important differences among them do not count. Genuine disagreements about work definition, therefore, are sometimes wrongly interpreted through this paradigm's fairness-unfairness lens—especially when honest disagreements are accompanied by tense debate. A female employee who insists, for example, that a company's advertising strategy is not appropriate for all ethnic segments in the marketplace might feel she is violating the code of assimilation upon which the paradigm is built. Moreover, if she were then to defend her opinion by citing, let us say, her personal knowledge of the ethnic group the company wanted to reach, she might risk being perceived as importing inappropriate attitudes into an organization that prides itself on being blind to cultural differences.

Workplace paradigms channel organizational thinking in powerful ways. By limiting the ability of employees to acknowledge openly their work-related but culturally based differences, the paradigm actually undermines the organization's capacity to learn about and improve its own strategies, processes, and practices. And it also keeps people from identifying strongly and personally with their work—a critical source of motivation and self-regulation in any business environment.

As an illustration of the paradigm's weaknesses, consider the case of Iversen Dunham, an international consulting firm that focuses on foreign and domestic economic-development policy. (Like all the examples in this article, the company is real, but its name is disguised.) Not long ago, the firm's managers asked us to help them understand why race relations had become a divisive issue precisely at a time when Iversen was receiving accolades for its diversity efforts. Indeed, other organizations had even begun to use the firm to benchmark their own diversity programs.

Iversen's diversity efforts had begun in the early 1970s, when senior managers decided to pursue greater racial and gender diversity in the firm's higher ranks. (The firm's leaders were strongly committed to the cause of social justice.) Women and people of color were hired and charted on career paths toward becoming project leaders. High performers among those who had left the firm were persuaded to return in senior roles. By 1989, about 50% of Iversen's project leaders and professionals were women, and 30% were people of color. The 13-member management committee, once exclusively white and male, included five women and four people of color. Additionally, Iversen had developed a strong contingent of foreign nationals.

It was at about this time, however, that tensions began to surface. Senior managers found it hard to believe that, after all the effort to create a fair and mutually respectful work community, some staff members could still be claiming that Iversen had racial discrimination problems. The management invited us to study the firm and deliver an outsider's assessment of its problem.

We had been inside the firm for only a short time when it became clear that Iversen's leaders viewed the dynamics of diversity through the lens of the discrimination-and-fairness paradigm. But where they saw racial discord, we discerned clashing approaches to the actual work of consulting. Why? Our research showed that tensions were strongest among midlevel project leaders. Surveys and interviews indicated that white project leaders welcomed demographic diversity as a general sign of progress but that they also thought the new employees were somehow changing the company, pulling it away from its original culture and its mission. Common criticisms were that African American and Hispanic staff made problems too complex by linking issues the organization had traditionally regarded as unrelated and that they brought on projects that seemed to require greater cultural sensitivity. White male project leaders also complained that their peers who were women and people of color were undermining one of Iversen's traditional strengths: its hard-core quantitative orientation. For instance, minority project leaders had suggested that Iversen consultants collect information and seek input from others in the client company besides senior managers—that is, from the rank and file and from middle managers. Some had urged Iversen to expand its consulting approach to include the gathering and analysis of qualitative data through interviewing and observation. Indeed, these project leaders had even challenged one of Iversen's long-standing, core assumptions: that the firm's reports were objective. They urged Iversen Dunham to recognize and address the subjective aspect of its analyses; the firm could, for example, include in its reports to clients dissenting Iversen views, if any existed.

For their part, project leaders who were women and people of color felt that they were not accorded the same level of authority to carry out that work as their white male peers. Moreover, they sensed that those peers were skeptical of their opinions, and they resented that doubts were not voiced openly.

Meanwhile, there also was some concern expressed about tension between white managers and nonwhite subordinates, who claimed they were being treated unfairly. But our analysis suggested that the manager-subordinate conflicts were not numerous enough

The Research

THIS ARTICLE IS BASED ON a three-part research effort that began in 1990. Our subject was diversity; but, more specifically, we sought to understand three management challenges under that heading. First, how do organizations successfully achieve and sustain racial and gender diversity in their executive and middle-management ranks? Second, what is the impact of diversity on an organization's practices, processes, and performance? And, finally, how do leaders influence whether diversity becomes an enhancing or detracting element in the organization?

Over the following six years, we worked particularly closely with three organizations that had attained a high degree of demographic diversity: a small urban law firm, a community bank, and a 200-person consulting firm. In addition, we studied nine other companies in varying stages of diversifying their workforces. The group included two financial-services firms, three *Fortune* 500 manufacturing companies, two midsize high-technology companies, a private foundation, and a university medical center. In each case, we based our analysis on interviews, surveys, archival data, and observation. It is from this work that the third paradigm for managing diversity emerged and with it our belief that old and limiting assumptions about the meaning of diversity must be abandoned before its true potential can be realized as a powerful way to increase organizational effectiveness.

to warrant the attention they were drawing from top management. We believed it was significant that senior managers found it easier to focus on this second type of conflict than on midlevel conflicts about project choice and project definition. Indeed, Iversen Dunham's focus seemed to be a result of the firm's reliance on its particular diversity paradigm and the emphasis on fairness and equality. It was relatively easy to diagnose problems in light of those concepts and to devise a solution: just get managers to treat their subordinates more fairly.

In contrast, it was difficult to diagnose peer-to-peer tensions in the framework of this model. Such conflicts were about the very nature of Iversen's work, not simply unfair treatment. Yes, they were related to identity-group affiliations, but they were not symptomatic of classic racism. It was Iversen's paradigm that led managers to interpret them as such. Remember, we were asked to assess what was supposed to be a racial discrimination problem. Iversen's discrimination-and-fairness paradigm had created a kind of cognitive blind spot; and, as a result, the company's leadership could not frame the problem accurately or solve it effectively. Instead, the company needed a cultural shift—it needed to grasp what to do with its diversity once it had achieved the numbers. If all Iversen Dunham employees were to contribute to the fullest extent, the company would need a paradigm that would encourage open and explicit discussion of what identity-group differences really mean and how they can be used as sources of individual and organizational effectiveness.

Today, mainly because of senior managers' resistance to such a cultural transformation, Iversen continues to struggle with the tensions arising from the diversity of its workforce.

The Access-and-Legitimacy Paradigm

In the competitive climate of the 1980s and 1990s, a new rhetoric and rationale for managing diversity emerged. If the discrimination-and-fairness paradigm can be said to have idealized assimilation and color- and gender-blind conformism, the access-and-legitimacy paradigm was predicated on the acceptance and celebration of differences. The underlying motivation of the access-and-legitimacy paradigm can be expressed this way:

> We are living in an increasingly multicultural country, and new ethnic groups are quickly gaining consumer power. Our company needs a demographically more diverse workforce to help us gain access to these differentiated segments. We need employees with multilingual skills in order to understand and serve our customers better and to gain legitimacy with them. Diversity isn't just fair; it makes business sense.

Where this paradigm has taken hold, organizations have pushed for access to—and legitimacy with—a more diverse clientele by matching the demographics of the organization to those of critical consumer or constituent groups. In some cases, the effort has led to substantial increases in organizational diversity. In investment banks, for example, municipal finance departments have long led corporate finance departments in pursuing demographic diversity because of the typical makeup of the administration of city halls and county boards. Many consumer-products companies that have used market segmentation based on gender, racial, and other demographic differences have also frequently created dedicated marketing positions for each segment. The paradigm has therefore led to new professional and managerial opportunities for women and people of color.

What are the common characteristics of organizations that have successfully used the access-and-legitimacy paradigm to increase their demographic diversity? There is but one: such companies almost always operate in a business environment in which there is increased diversity among customers, clients, or the labor pool—and therefore a clear opportunity or an imminent threat to the company.

Again, the paradigm has its strengths. Its market-based motivation and the potential for competitive advantage that it suggests are often qualities an entire company can understand and therefore support. But the paradigm is perhaps more notable for its limitations. In their pursuit of niche markets, access-and-legitimacy organizations tend to emphasize the role of cultural differences in a company without really analyzing those differences to see how they actually affect the work that is done. Whereas discrimination-and-fairness leaders are too quick to subvert differences in the interest of preserving harmony, access-and-legitimacy leaders are too quick to push staff with niche capabilities into differentiated pigeonholes without trying to understand what those capabilities really are and how they could be integrated into the company's mainstream work. To illustrate our point, we present the case of Access Capital.

Access Capital International is a U.S. investment bank that in the early 1980s launched an aggressive plan to expand into Europe. Initially, however, Access encountered serious problems opening offices in international markets; the people from the United States who were installed abroad lacked credibility, were ignorant of local cultural norms and market conditions, and simply couldn't seem to connect with native clients. Access responded by hiring Europeans who had attended North American business schools and by assigning them in teams to the foreign offices. This strategy was a marked success. Before long, the leaders of Access could take enormous pride in the fact that their European operations were highly profitable and staffed by a truly international corps of professionals. They took to calling the company "the best investment bank in the world."

Several years passed. Access's foreign offices continued to thrive, but some leaders were beginning to sense that the company was not fully benefiting from its diversity efforts. Indeed, some even suspected that the bank had made itself vulnerable because of how it had chosen to manage diversity. A senior executive from the United States explains:

> If the French team all resigned tomorrow, what would we do? I'm not sure what we *could* do! We've never attempted to learn what these differences and cultural competencies really are, how they change the process of doing business. What is the German country team actually doing? We don't know. We know they're good, but we don't know the subtleties of how they do what they do. We assumed—and I think correctly—that culture makes a difference, but that's about as far as we went. We hired Europeans with American M.B.A.'s because we didn't know why we couldn't do business in Europe—we just assumed there was something cultural about why we couldn't connect. And ten years later, we still don't know what it is. If we knew, then perhaps we could take it and teach it. Which part of the investment banking process is universal and which part of it draws upon particular cultural competencies? What are the commonalities and differences? I may not be German, but maybe I could do better at understanding what it means to be an American doing business in Germany. Our company's biggest failing is that the department heads in London and the directors of the various country teams have never talked about these cultural identity issues openly. We knew enough to *use* people's cultural strengths, as it were, but we never seemed to learn from them.

Access's story makes an important point about the main limitation of the access-and-legitimacy paradigm: under its influence, the motivation for diversity usually emerges from very immediate and often crisis-oriented needs for access and legitimacy—in this case, the need to broker deals in European markets. However, once the organization appears to be achieving its goal, the leaders seldom go on to identify and analyze the culturally based skills, beliefs, and practices that worked so well. Nor do they consider how the organization can incorporate and learn from those skills, beliefs, or practices in order to capitalize on diversity in the long run.

Under the access-and-legitimacy paradigm, it was as if the bank's country teams had become little spin-off companies in their own right, doing their own exotic, slightly mysterious cultural-diversity thing in a niche market of their own, using competencies that for some reason could not become more fully integrated into the larger organization's understanding of itself. Difference was valued within Access Capital—hence the development of country teams in the first place—but not valued enough that the organization would try to integrate it into the very core of its culture and into its business practices.

Finally, the access-and-legitimacy paradigm can leave some employees feeling exploited. Many organizations using this paradigm have diversified only in those areas in which they interact with particular niche-market segments. In time, many individuals recruited for this function have come to feel devalued and used as they begin to sense that opportunities in other parts of the organization are closed to them. Often the larger organization regards the experience of these employees as more limited or specialized, even though many of them in fact started their careers in the mainstream market before moving to special markets where their cultural backgrounds were a recognized asset. Also, many of these people say that when companies have needed to downsize or narrow their marketing focus, it is the special departments that are often the first to go. That situation creates tenuous and ultimately untenable career paths for employees in the special departments.

The Emerging Paradigm: Connecting Diversity to Work Perspectives

Recently, in the course of our research, we have encountered a small number of organizations that, having relied initially on one of the above paradigms to guide their diversity efforts, have come to believe that they are not making the most of their own pluralism. These organizations, like Access Capital, recognize that employees frequently make decisions and choices at work that draw upon their cultural background—choices made because of their identity-group affiliations. The companies have also developed an outlook on diversity that enables them to *incorporate* employees' perspectives into the main work of the organization and to enhance work by rethinking primary tasks and redefining markets, products, strategies, missions, business practices, and even cultures. Such companies are using the learning-and-effectiveness paradigm for managing diversity and, by doing so, are tapping diversity's true benefits.

A case in point is Dewey & Levin, a small public-interest law firm located in a northeastern U.S. city. Although Dewey & Levin had long been a profitable practice, by the mid-1980s its all-white legal staff had become concerned that the women they represented in employment-related disputes were exclusively white. The firm's attorneys viewed that fact as a deficiency in light of their mandate to advocate on behalf of all women. Using the thinking behind the access-and-legitimacy paradigm, they also saw it as bad for business.

Shortly thereafter, the firm hired a Hispanic female attorney. The partners' hope, simply put, was that she would bring in clients from her own community and also demonstrate the firm's commitment to representing all women. But something even bigger than that happened. The new attorney introduced ideas to Dewey & Levin about what kinds of cases it should take on. Senior managers were open to those ideas and pursued them with great success. More women of color were hired, and they, too, brought fresh perspectives. The firm now pursues cases that its previously all-white legal staff would not have thought relevant or appropriate because the link between the firm's mission and the employment issues involved in the cases would not have been obvious to them. For example, the firm has pursued precedent-setting litigation that challenges English-only policies—an area that it once would have ignored because such policies did not fall under the purview of traditional affirmative-action work. Yet it now sees a link between English-only policies and employment issues for a large group of women—primarily recent immigrants—whom it had previously failed to serve adequately. As one of the white principals explains, the demographic composition of Dewey & Levin "has affected the work in terms of expanding notions of what are [relevant] issues and taking on issues and framing them in creative ways that would have never been done [with an all-white staff]. It's really changed the substance—and in that sense enhanced the quality—of our work."

Dewey & Levin's increased business success has reinforced its commitment to diversity. In addition, people of color at the firm uniformly report feeling respected, not simply "brought along as window dressing." Many of the new attorneys say their perspectives are heard with a kind of openness and interest they have never experienced before in a work setting. Not surprisingly, the firm has had little difficulty attracting and retaining a competent and diverse professional staff.

If the discrimination-and-fairness paradigm is organized around the theme of assimilation—in which the aim is to achieve a demographically representative workforce whose members treat one another exactly the same—then the access-and-legitimacy paradigm can be regarded as coalescing around an almost opposite concept: differentiation, in which the objective is to place different people where their demographic characteristics match those of important constituents and markets.

The emerging paradigm, in contrast to both, organizes itself around the overarching theme of integration. Assimilation goes too far in pursuing sameness. Differentiation, as we have shown, overshoots in the other direction. The new model for managing diversity transcends both. Like the fairness paradigm, it promotes equal opportunity for all individuals. And like the access paradigm, it acknowledges cultural differences among people and recognizes the value in those differences. Yet this new model for managing diversity lets the organization internalize differences among employees so that it learns and grows because of them. Indeed, with the model fully in place, members of the organization can say, We are all on the same team, *with* our differences—not *despite* them.

Eight Preconditions for Making the Paradigm Shift

Dewey & Levin may be atypical in its eagerness to open itself up to change and engage in a long-term transformation process. We remain convinced, however, that unless organizations that are currently in the grip of the other two paradigms can revise their view of diversity so as to avoid cognitive blind spots, opportunities will be missed, tensions will most likely be misdiagnosed, and companies will continue to find the potential benefits of diversity elusive.

Hence the question arises: What is it about the law firm of Dewey & Levin and other emerging third-paradigm companies that enables them to make the most of their diversity? Our research suggests that there are eight preconditions that help to position organizations to use identity-group differences in the service of organizational learning, growth, and renewal.

1. The leadership must understand that a diverse workforce will embody different perspectives and approaches to work, and must truly value variety of opinion and insight. We know of a financial services company that once assumed that the only successful sales model was one that utilized aggressive, rapid-fire cold calls. (Indeed, its incentive system rewarded salespeople in large part for the number of calls made.) An internal review of the company's diversity initiatives, however, showed that the company's first- and third-most-profitable employees were women who were most likely to use a sales technique based on the slow but sure building of relationships. The company's top management has now made the link between different identity groups and different approaches to how work gets done and has come to see that there is more than one right way to get positive results.

2. The leadership must recognize both the learning opportuni-ties and the challenges that the expression of different perspec-tives presents for an organization. In other words, the second precondition is a leadership that is committed to persevering during the long process of learning and relearning that the new paradigm requires.

3. The organizational culture must create an expectation of high standards of performance from everyone. Such a culture isn't one that expects less from some employees than from others. Some or-ganizations expect women and people of color to underperform—a negative assumption that too often becomes a self-fulfilling proph-ecy. To move to the third paradigm, a company must believe that all its members can and should contribute fully.

4. The organizational culture must stimulate personal devel-opment. Such a culture brings out people's full range of useful knowledge and skills—usually through the careful design of jobs that allow people to grow and develop but also through training and education programs.

5. The organizational culture must encourage openness. Such a culture instills a high tolerance for debate and supports constructive conflict on work-related matters.

6. The culture must make workers feel valued. If this precondition is met, workers feel committed to—and empowered within—the organization and therefore feel comfortable taking the initiative to apply their skills and experiences in new ways to enhance their job performance.

7. The organization must have a well-articulated and widely un-derstood mission. Such a mission enables people to be clear about what the company is trying to accomplish. It grounds and guides discussions about work-related changes that staff members might suggest. Being clear about the company's mission helps keep discussions about work differences from degenerating into debates about the validity of people's perspectives. A clear mission provides a focal point that keeps the discussion centered on accomplishment of goals.

8. The organization must have a relatively egalitarian, nonbureaucratic structure. It's important to have a structure that promotes the exchange of ideas and welcomes constructive challenges to the usual way of doing things—from any employee with valuable experience. Forward-thinking leaders in bureaucratic organizations must retain the organization's efficiency-promoting control systems and chains of command while finding ways to reshape the change-resisting mind-set of the classic bureaucratic model. They need to separate the enabling elements of bureaucracy (the ability to get things done) from the disabling elements of bureaucracy (those that create resistance to experimentation).

First Interstate Bank: A Paradigm Shift in Progress

All eight preconditions do not have to be in place in order to begin a shift from the first or second diversity orientations toward the learning-and-effectiveness paradigm. But most should be. First Interstate Bank, a midsize bank operating in a midwestern city, illustrates this point.

First Interstate, admittedly, is not a typical bank. Its client base is a minority community, and its mission is expressly to serve that base through "the development of a highly talented workforce." The bank is unique in other ways: its leadership welcomes constructive criticism; its structure is relatively egalitarian and nonbureaucratic; and its culture is open-minded. Nevertheless, First Interstate had long enforced a policy that loan officers had to hold college degrees. Those without were hired only for support-staff jobs and were never promoted beyond or outside support functions.

Two years ago, however, the support staff began to challenge the policy. Many of them had been with First Interstate for many years and, with the company's active support, had improved their skills through training. Others had expanded their skills on the job, again with the bank's encouragement, learning to run credit checks, prepare presentations for clients, and even calculate the algorithms necessary for many loan decisions. As a result, some people on the support staff were doing many of the same tasks as loan officers. Why, then, they wondered, couldn't they receive commensurate rewards in title and compensation?

This questioning led to a series of contentious meetings between the support staff and the bank's senior managers. It soon became clear that the problem called for managing diversity—diversity based not on race or gender but on class. The support personnel were uniformly from lower socioeconomic communities than were the college-educated loan officers. Regardless, the principle was the same as for race-or gender-based diversity problems. The support staff had different ideas about how the work of the bank should be done. They argued that those among them with the requisite skills should be allowed to rise through the ranks to professional positions, and they believed their ideas were not being heard or accepted.

Their beliefs challenged assumptions that the company's leadership had long held about which employees should have the authority to deal with customers and about how much responsibility administrative employees should ultimately receive. In order to take up this challenge, the bank would have to be open to exploring the requirements that a new perspective would impose on it. It would need to consider the possibility of mapping out an educational and career path for people without degrees—a path that could put such workers on the road to becoming loan officers. In other words, the leadership would have to transform itself willingly and embrace fluidity in policies that in times past had been clearly stated and unquestioningly held.

Today the bank's leadership is undergoing just such a transformation. The going, however, is far from easy. The bank's senior managers now must look beyond the tensions and acrimony sparked by the debate over differing work perspectives and consider the bank's new direction an important learning and growth opportunity.

Shift Complete: Third-Paradigm Companies in Action

First Interstate is a shift in progress; but, in addition to Dewey & Levin, there are several organizations we know of for which the shift is complete. In these cases, company leaders have played a critical role as facilitators and tone setters. We have observed in particular that in organizations that have adopted the new perspective, leaders and managers—and, following in their tracks, employees in general—are taking four kinds of action.

They are making the mental connection

First, in organizations that have adopted the new perspective, the leaders are actively seeking opportunities to explore how identity-group differences affect relationships among workers and affect the way work gets done. They are investing considerable time and energy in understanding how identity-group memberships take on social meanings in the organization and how those meanings manifest themselves in the way work is defined, assigned, and accomplished. When there is no proactive search to understand, then learning from diversity, if it happens at all, can occur only reactively—that is, in response to diversity-related crises.

The situation at Iversen Dunham illustrates the missed opportunities resulting from that scenario. Rather than seeing differences in the way project leaders defined and approached their work as an opportunity to gain new insights and develop new approaches to achieving its mission, the firm remained entrenched in its traditional ways, able to arbitrate such differences only by thinking about what was fair and what was racist. With this quite limited view of the role race can play in an organization, discussions about the topic become fraught with fear and defensiveness, and everyone misses out on insights about how race might influence work in positive ways.

A second case, however, illustrates how some leaders using the new paradigm have been able to envision—and make—the connection between cultural diversity and the company's work. A vice president of Mastiff, a large national insurance company, received a complaint from one of the managers in her unit, an African American

67

man. The manager wanted to demote an African American woman he had hired for a leadership position from another Mastiff division just three months before. He told the vice president he was profoundly disappointed with the performance of his new hire.

"I hired her because I was pretty certain she had tremendous leadership skill," he said. "I knew she had a management style that was very open and empowering. I was also sure she'd have a great impact on the rest of the management team. But she hasn't done any of that."

Surprised, the vice president tried to find out from him what he thought the problem was, but she was not getting any answers that she felt really defined or illuminated the root of the problem. Privately, it puzzled her that someone would decide to demote a 15-year veteran of the company—and a minority woman at that—so soon after bringing her to his unit.

The vice president probed further. In the course of the conversation, the manager happened to mention that he knew the new employee from church and was familiar with the way she handled leadership there and in other community settings. In those less formal situations, he had seen her perform as an extremely effective, sensitive, and influential leader.

That is when the vice president made an interpretive leap. "If that's what you know about her," the vice president said to the manager, "then the question for us is, why can't she bring those skills to work here?" The vice president decided to arrange a meeting with all three present to ask this very question directly. In the meeting, the African American woman explained, "I didn't think I would last long if I acted that way here. My personal style of leadership—that particular style—works well if you have the permission to do it fully; then you can just do it and not have to look over your shoulder."

Pointing to the manager who had planned to fire her, she added, "He's right. The style of leadership I use outside this company can definitely be effective. But I've been at Mastiff for 15 years. I know this organization, and I know if I brought that piece of myself—if I became that authentic—I just wouldn't survive here."

What this example illustrates is that the vice president's learning-and-effectiveness paradigm led her to explore and then make the link between cultural diversity and work style. What was occurring, she realized, was a mismatch between the cultural background of the recently promoted woman and the cultural environment of her work setting. It had little to do with private attitudes or feelings, or gender issues, or some inherent lack of leadership ability. The source of the underperformance was that the newly promoted woman had a certain style and the organization's culture did not support her in expressing it comfortably. The vice president's paradigm led her to ask new questions and to seek out new information, but, more important, it also led her to interpret existing information differently.

The two senior managers began to realize that part of the African American woman's inability to see herself as a leader at work was that she had for so long been undervalued in the organization. And, in a sense, she had become used to splitting herself off from who she was in her own community. In the 15 years she had been at Mastiff, she had done her job well as an individual contributor, but she had never received any signals that her bosses wanted her to draw on her cultural competencies in order to lead effectively.

They are legitimating open discussion

Leaders and managers who have adopted the new paradigm are taking the initiative to "green light" open discussion about how identity-group memberships inform and influence an employee's experience and the organization's behavior. They are encouraging people to make *explicit* use of background cultural experience and the pools of knowledge gained outside the organization to inform and enhance their work. Individuals often do use their cultural competencies at work, but in a closeted, almost embarrassed, way. The unfortunate result is that the opportunity for collective and organizational learning and improvement is lost.

The case of a Chinese woman who worked as a chemist at Torinno Food Company illustrates this point. Linda was part of a product development group at Torinno when a problem arose with the flavoring of a new soup. After the group had made a number of scientific attempts to correct the problem, Linda came up with the solution by "setting aside my chemistry and drawing on my under-standing of Chinese cooking." She did not, however, share with her colleagues—all of them white males—the real source of her inspira-tion for the solution for fear that it would set her apart or that they might consider her unprofessional. Overlaid on the cultural issue, of course, was a gender issue (women cooking) as well as a work-family issue (women doing *home* cooking in a chemistry lab). All of these themes had erected unspoken boundaries that Linda knew could be career-damaging for her to cross. After solving the problem, she sim-ply went back to the so-called scientific way of doing things.

Senior managers at Torinno Foods in fact had made a substan-tial commitment to diversifying the workforce through a program designed to teach employees to value the contributions of all its members. Yet Linda's perceptions indicate that, in the actual day-to-day context of work, the program had failed—and in precisely one of those areas where it would have been important for it to have worked. It had failed to affirm someone's identity-group experiences as a legitimate source of insight into her work. It is likely that this organization will miss future opportunities to take full advantage of the talent of employees such as Linda. When people believe that they must suggest and apply their ideas covertly, the organization also misses opportunities to discuss, debate, refine, and build on those ideas fully. In addition, because individuals like Linda will continue to think that they must hide parts of themselves in order to fit in, they will find it difficult to engage fully not only in their work but also in their workplace relationships. That kind of situation can breed resentment and misunderstanding, fueling tensions that can further obstruct productive work relationships.

They actively work against forms of dominance and subordination that inhibit full contribution

Companies in which the third paradigm is emerging have leaders and managers who take responsibility for removing the barriers that block employees from using the full range of their competen-cies, cultural or otherwise. Racism, homophobia, sexism, and sexual harassment are the most obvious forms of dominance that decrease individual and organizational effectiveness—and third-paradigm leaders have zero tolerance for them. In addition, the leaders are aware that organizations can create their own unique patterns of dominance and subordination based on the presumed superiority and entitlement of some groups over others. It is not uncommon, for instance, to find organizations in which one functional area considers itself better than another. Members of the presumed inferior group frequently describe the organization in the very terms used by those who experience identity-group discrimination. Regardless of the source of the oppression, the result is diminished performance and commitment from employees.

What can leaders do to prevent those kinds of behaviors beyond explicitly forbidding any forms of dominance? They can and should test their own assumptions about the competencies of all members of the workforce because negative assumptions are often unconsciously communicated in powerful—albeit nonverbal—ways. For example, senior managers at Delta Manufacturing had for years allowed productivity and quality at their inner-city plants to lag well behind the levels of other plants. When the company's chief executive officer began to question why the problem was never addressed, he came to realize that, in his heart, he had believed that inner-city workers, most of whom were African American or Hispanic, were not capable of doing better than subpar. In the end, the CEO and his senior management team were able to reverse their reasoning and take responsibility for improving the situation. The result was a sharp increase in the performance of the inner-city plants and a message to the entire organization about the capabilities of its entire workforce.

At Mastiff, the insurance company discussed earlier, the vice president and her manager decided to work with the recently promoted African American woman rather than demote her. They realized that their unit was really a pocket inside the larger organization: they did not have to wait for the rest of the organization to make a paradigm shift in order for their particular unit to change. So they met again to think about how to create conditions within their unit that would move the woman toward seeing her leadership position as encompassing all her skills. They assured her that her authentic style of leadership was precisely what they wanted her to bring to the job. They wanted her to be able to use whatever aspects of herself she thought would make her more effective in her work because the whole purpose was to do the job effectively, not to fit some preset traditional formula of how to behave. They let her know that, as a management team, they would try to adjust and change and support her. And they would deal with whatever consequences resulted from her exercising her decision rights in new ways.

Another example of this line of action—working against forms of dominance and subordination to enable full contribution—is the way the CEO of a major chemical company modified the attendance rules for his company's annual strategy conference. In the past, the conference had been attended only by senior executives, a relatively homogeneous group of white men. The company had been working hard on increasing the representation of women and people of color in its ranks, and the CEO could have left it at that. But he reckoned that, unless steps were taken, it would be ten years before the conferences tapped into the insights and perspectives of his newly diverse workforce. So he took the bold step of opening the conference to people from across all levels of the hierarchy, bringing together a diagonal slice of the organization. He also asked the conference organizers to come up with specific interventions, such as small group meetings before the larger session, to ensure that the new attendees would be comfortable enough to enter discussions. The result was that strategy-conference participants heard a much broader, richer, and livelier discussion about future scenarios for the company.

They are making sure that organizational trust stays intact

Few things are faster at killing a shift to a new way of thinking about diversity than feelings of broken trust. Therefore, managers of organizations that are successfully shifting to the learning-and-effectiveness paradigm take one more step: they make sure their organizations remain "safe" places for employees to be themselves. These managers recognize that tensions naturally arise as an organization begins to make room for diversity, starts to experiment with process and product ideas, and learns to reappraise its mission in light of suggestions from newly empowered constituents in the company. But as people put more of themselves out and open up about new feelings and ideas, the dynamics of the learning-and-effectiveness paradigm can produce temporary vulnerabilities. Managers who have helped their organizations make the change successfully have consistently demonstrated their commitment to the process and to all employees by setting a tone of honest discourse, by acknowledging tensions, and by resolving them sensitively and swiftly.

Our research over the past six years indicates that one cardinal limitation is at the root of companies' inability to attain the expected performance benefits of higher levels of diversity: the leadership's vision of the purpose of a diversified workforce. We have described the two most dominant orientations toward diversity and some of their consequences and limitations, together with a new framework for understanding and managing diversity. The learning-and-effectiveness paradigm we have outlined here is, undoubtedly, still in an emergent phase in those few organizations that embody it. We expect that as more organizations take on the challenge of truly engaging their diversity, new and unforeseen dilemmas will arise. Thus, perhaps more than anything else, a shift toward this paradigm requires a high-level commitment to learning more about the environment, structure, and tasks of one's organization, and giving improvement-generating change greater priority than the security of what is familiar. This is not an easy challenge, but we remain convinced that unless organizations take this step, any diversity initiative will fall short of fulfilling its rich promise.

Originally published in September–October 1996. Reprint 96510

.

Navigating the Cultural Minefield

by Erin Meyer

WHEN AARON ARRIVED IN MOSCOW to take charge of the manufacturing plant his Israeli-owned company had just purchased, he expected to settle in quickly. Although he'd grown up in Tel Aviv, his parents were Russian-born, so he knew the culture and spoke the language well. He'd been highly successful managing Israeli teams and had led a large organization in Canada. Yet six months into his new job, he was still struggling to supervise his team in Moscow. What, specifically, was he doing wrong?

Answering such questions isn't easy, as I've learned from 16 years studying the effects of cultural differences on business success. Although there's been a great deal of research and writing on the subject, much of it fails to present a sufficiently nuanced picture that can be of real use to managers working internationally or with foreign colleagues. As a result, it's all too common to rely on clichés, stereotyping people from different cultures on just one or two dimensions—the Japanese are hierarchical, for example, or the French communicate in subtle ways. This can lead to oversimplified and erroneous assumptions—the Japanese always make top-down decisions, or the French are indirect when giving negative feedback. It then comes as a surprise when your French colleague bluntly criticizes your shortcomings, or when your Japanese clients want buy-in from the cook and the cleaner before reaching a decision.

Time and again, I find that even experienced and cosmopolitan managers have faulty expectations about how people from other cultures operate. The truth is that culture is too complex to be measured meaningfully along just one or two dimensions.

To help managers like Aaron negotiate this complexity, I have built on the work of many in my field to develop a tool called the Culture Map. It is made up of eight scales representing the management behaviors where cultural gaps are most common. By comparing the position of one nationality relative to another on each scale, the user can decode how culture influences day-to-day collaboration. In the following pages, I present the tool, show how it can help you, and discuss the challenges in applying it.

The Culture Map

The eight scales on the map are based on decades of academic research into culture from multiple perspectives. To this foundation I have added my own work, which has been validated by extensive interviews with thousands of executives who have confirmed or corrected my findings. The scales and their metrics are:

Communicating

When we say that someone is a good communicator, what do we actually mean? The responses differ wildly from society to society. I compare cultures along the Communicating scale by measuring the degree to which they are high- or low-context, a metric developed by the American anthropologist Edward Hall. In low-context cultures, good communication is precise, simple, explicit, and clear. Messages are understood at face value. Repetition is appreciated for purposes of clarification, as is putting messages in writing. In high-context cultures, communication is sophisticated, nuanced, and layered. Messages are often implied but not plainly stated. Less is put in writing, more is left open to interpretation, and understanding may depend on reading between the lines.

Idea in Brief

As we increasingly work with colleagues and clients who come from all parts of the world, it is vital to understand how cultural differences affect business. Yet too often we rely on clichés and stereotypes that lead us to false assumptions. To help managers negotiate the complexity of an international work team, INSEAD professor Erin Meyer has developed a tool called the Culture Map, which plots the positions of numerous nationalities along eight behavior scales: Communicating, Evaluating, Persuading, Leading, Deciding, Trusting, Disagreeing, and Scheduling. Meyer suggests that comparing the relative positions of different nationalities along

these scales can help us decode how culture influences workplace dynamics. She adds four important rules: Don't underestimate the challenge. Management and work styles stem from lifelong habits that can be hard to change. Apply multiple perspectives. Be aware of your own expectations and behaviors, but also consider how members of other cultures perceive you and fellow teammates. Find the positive in other approaches. The differences that people of varied backgrounds bring to a work group can be great assets. Continually adjust your position. Be prepared to keep adapting your behavior to meld with the styles of your colleagues.

Evaluating

All cultures believe that criticism should be given constructively, but the definition of "constructive" varies greatly. This scale measures a preference for frank versus diplomatic negative feedback. Evaluating is often confused with Communicating, but many countries have different positions on the two scales. The French, for example, are high-context (implicit) communicators relative to Americans, yet they are more direct in their criticism. Spaniards and Mexicans are at the same context level, but the Spanish are much more frank when providing negative feedback. This scale is my own work.

Persuading

The ways in which you persuade others and the kinds of arguments you find convincing are deeply rooted in your culture's philosophical, religious, and educational assumptions and attitudes. The traditional way to compare countries along this scale is to assess how they balance holistic and specific thought patterns. Typically, a Western executive will break down an argument into a sequence of distinct components (specific thinking), while Asian managers tend to show how the components all fit together (holistic thinking). Beyond that, people from southern European and Germanic cultures tend to find deductive arguments (what I refer to as principles-first arguments) most persuasive, whereas American and British managers are more likely to be influenced by inductive logic (what I call applications-first logic). The research into specific and holistic cognitive patterns was conducted by Richard Nisbett, an American professor of social psychology, and the deductive/inductive element is my own work.

Leading

This scale measures the degree of respect and deference shown to authority figures, placing countries on a spectrum from egalitarian to hierarchical. The Leading scale is based partly on the concept of power distance, first researched by the Dutch social psychologist Geert Hofstede, who conducted 100,000 management surveys at IBM in the 1970s. It also draws on the work of Wharton School professor Robert House and his colleagues in their GLOBE (global leadership and organizational behavior effectiveness) study of 62 societies.

Deciding

This scale, based on my own work, measures the degree to which a culture is consensus-minded. We often assume that the most egalitarian cultures will also be the most democratic, while the most hierarchical ones will allow the boss to make unilateral decisions. This isn't always the case. Germans are more hierarchical than Americans, but more likely than their U.S. colleagues to build group agreement before making decisions. The Japanese are both strongly hierarchical and strongly consensus-minded.

Trusting

Cognitive trust (from the head) can be contrasted with affective trust (from the heart). In task-based cultures, trust is built cognitively through work. If we collaborate well, prove ourselves reliable, and respect one another's contributions, we come to feel mutual trust. In a relationship-based society, trust is a result of weaving a strong affective connection. If we spend time laughing and relaxing together, get to know one another on a personal level, and feel a mutual liking, then we establish trust. Many people have researched this topic; Roy Chua and Michael Morris, for example, wrote a landmark paper on the different approaches to trust in the United States and China. I have drawn on this work in developing my metric.

Disagreeing

Everyone believes that a little open disagreement is healthy, right? The recent American business literature certainly confirms this viewpoint. But different cultures actually have very different ideas about how productive confrontation is for a team or an organization. This scale measures tolerance for open disagreement and inclination to see it as either helpful or harmful to collegial relationships. This is my own work.

Scheduling

All businesses follow agendas and timetables, but in some cultures people strictly adhere to the schedule, whereas in others, they treat it as a suggestion. This scale assesses how much value is placed on operating in a structured, linear fashion versus being flexible and reactive. It is based on the "monochronic" and "polychronic" distinction formalized by Edward Hall.

The Culture Map shows positions along these eight scales for a large number of countries, based on surveys and interviews. These profiles reflect, of course, the value systems of a society at large, not those of all the individuals in it, so if you plot yourself on the map, you might find that some of your preferences differ from those of your culture.

Let's go back to my friend Aaron (who, like other managers profiled later, is not identified by his real name). Aaron used the map to uncover the roots of his difficulties managing his Moscow team. As you can see from the exhibit "Comparing management cultures: Israel vs. Russia," there are plenty of cultural similarities between

Israelis and Russians. For example, both value flexible rather than linear scheduling, both accept and appreciate open disagreement, and both approach issues of trust through a relationship lens. But there are also big gaps. For instance, Russians strongly value hierarchy, whereas Israelis are more egalitarian. This suggests that some of Aaron's management practices, developed through his experiences in Israel and Canada, may have been misunderstood by—and demotivating to—his Russian team.

As Aaron considered the large gap on the Leading scale, he began to think about how he'd been encouraged as a child to disagree openly with authority figures in his family and community—a stark

Comparing management cultures: Israel vs. Russia

This Culture Map plots the Israeli and Russian business cultures on eight behavior scales. The profiles are drawn from surveys and interviews of managers from the two countries. While there are many points of similarity, Russians and Israelis diverge with respect to the ways in which they persuade, lead, and decide.

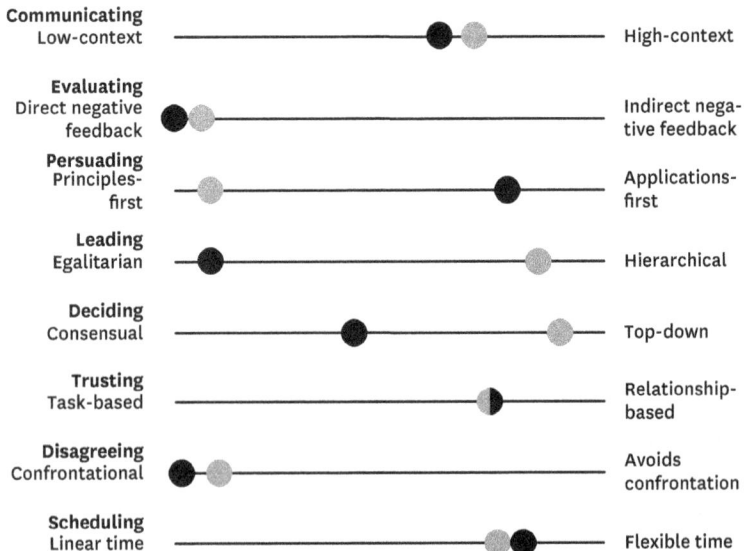

contrast to the Russian tradition of expecting young people to show deep respect and deference to their elders. "In Israel, the boss is just one of the guys," he reflected. "But in Russia, when I try to push decision making down and insist that someone on my team is better positioned to make a decision than I am, it often suggests weak leadership." One of the specific practices getting him into trouble was his tendency to e-mail employees at lower levels of the company without passing through the hierarchical chain or cc'ing their direct bosses; he now understood why the practice made his middle managers so angry.

Sometimes it's fairly easy to bridge the cultural gaps revealed by the mapping process. Aaron found that simply stopping the direct e-mails and going through official channels had a big impact. But some differences are more difficult to overcome, and as you manage across them, it's important to respect the four rules I discuss next. They apply to all the scales, but I'll continue to focus on Leading.

Rule 1: Don't Underestimate the Challenge

Management styles stem from habits developed over a lifetime, which makes them hard to change. Here's a good example: In 2010 Heineken, the Dutch brewing company, purchased a big operation in Monterrey, Mexico, and a large number of Mexican employees are now based at its Amsterdam headquarters. One of these is Carlos, the director of marketing for the Dos Equis brand, who admits that he struggled during his first year in the position:

"It is incredible to manage Dutch people, and nothing like my experience leading Mexican teams. I'll schedule a meeting to roll out a new process, and during it, my team starts challenging the process, taking us in various unexpected directions, ignoring my process altogether, and paying no attention to the fact that they work for me. Sometimes I just watch them astounded. Where is the respect?

"I know this treating everyone as pure equals is the Dutch way, so I keep quiet and try to be patient. But often I just feel like getting down on my knees and pleading, 'Dear colleagues, in case you have forgotten: I-am-the-boss.'"

It didn't take long for Carlos to realize that the leadership skills he had built over the previous decade in Mexico, where more deference to authority is the norm, were not going to transfer easily to the Netherlands. Succeeding would depend on taking an entirely different approach and making ongoing adjustments over the long term. "I realized I was going to need to unlearn many of the techniques that had made me so successful in Mexico and develop others from the ground up," he said.

Rule 2: Apply Multiple Perspectives

If you are leading a global team with, say, Brazilian, Korean, and Indian members, it isn't enough to recognize how your culture perceives each of the others. You need to understand how the Koreans perceive the Indians, how the Indians perceive the Brazilians, and so on, and manage across the map. As you learn to look through multiple lenses, you may see that on some scales the Brazilians, for example, view the Indians in a very different way than the Koreans do.

Let's return to the case of Heineken. A manager from China who had recently moved to Monterrey assessed the Mexicans this way: "They really think everyone is equal. No matter your age, rank, or title, everyone gets a voice here. They want us to call them by their first name and disagree with them in public. For a Chinese person, this is not at all comfortable." His take on Mexican culture, of course, was nothing like Carlos's and actually sounded like Carlos's view of Dutch culture.

The point is that where a culture falls on a scale doesn't in itself mean anything. What matters is the position of one country relative to another. On the Leading scale, Mexico falls somewhere between the Netherlands (one of the most egalitarian countries in the world) and China (strongly hierarchical), and the distances separating them led to these completely contradictory perceptions.

Rule 3: Find the Positive in Other Approaches

When looking at how other cultures work, people tend to see the negative. Steve, an Australian running the business unit of a textile company in China, admits that when he first arrived in the country, he was deeply critical of local leadership practices. The prevailing view, he found, was that "the boss is always right, and even when the boss is very wrong, he is still right." Having been raised to regard a fixed social hierarchy as an inhumane system, subverting individual freedom, he was uncomfortable in his new environment.

Yet Steve gradually came to understand and respect the Chinese system of reciprocal obligation. "In the Confucian concept of hierarchy," he says, "it's important to think not just about the lower-level person's responsibility to follow, but also about the responsibility of the higher person to protect and care for those under him. And there is great beauty in giving a clear instruction and watching your competent and enthusiastic team willingly attack the project without pushing back."

Carlos at Heineken underwent a similar transformation. He developed an appreciation for his Dutch colleagues' more egalitarian work style when he started to focus on the creative ideas generated and the problems averted because his employees felt so comfortable openly challenging his views.

Sometimes cultural diversity can cause inefficiency and confusion. But if the team leader clearly understands how people from varied backgrounds behave, he or she can turn differences into the team's greatest assets. As Steve explains, "Now that I run a Chinese-Australian operation, I think carefully about how to take advantage of the various styles on the team. Sometimes I really need a couple of experts on my staff to tear my ideas apart to ensure that we get the best solution. Sometimes we are under time pressure and I need streamlined reactivity. My overriding goal is to have a complex enough understanding of the various strengths on the team so I can choose the best subteam for each task."

Rule 4: Adjust, and Readjust, Your Position

More and more teams are made up of diverse and globally dispersed members. So as a leader, you'll frequently have to tweak or adapt your own style to better mesh with your working partners. It's not enough to shift to a new position on a single scale; you'll need to widen your comfort zone so that you can move more fluidly back and forth along all eight.

During his first year in Russia, Aaron invested significant time in watching how the most successful local leaders motivated their staff members. He learned step-by-step to be more of a director and less of a facilitator. "It worked," he said, "but when I returned to Israel, I was then accused of centralizing too much. Without realizing it, I had brought what I had developed in Russia back home." Gradually Aaron got better at adapting his behavior to the individuals and context at hand.

As Aaron, Carlos, and Steve all learned, to navigate cultural differences, you might need to go back to square one. Consider which leadership styles are most effective in disparate localities and with people of diverse nationalities. Check your knee-jerk tendencies— and learn to laugh at them. Then practice leading in a wide variety of ways to better motivate and mobilize groups who follow in different ways from the folks back home.

Whether we work in Düsseldorf or Dubai, Brasília or Beijing, New York or New Delhi, we are all part of a global network. This is true in the office or at a meeting, and it is true virtually, when we connect via e-mail, videoconference, Skype, or phone. Today success depends on the ability to navigate the wild variations in the ways people from different societies think, lead, and get things done. By sidestepping common stereotypes and learning to decode the behavior of other cultures along all the scales, we can avoid giving (and taking!) offense and better capitalize on the strengths of increased diversity.

Originally published in May 2014. Reprint R1405K

Values in Tension

Ethics Away from Home. *by Thomas Donaldson*

WHEN WE LEAVE HOME and cross our nation's boundaries, moral clarity often blurs. Without a backdrop of shared attitudes, and without familiar laws and judicial procedures that define standards of ethical conduct, certainty is elusive. Should a company invest in a foreign country where civil and political rights are violated? Should a company go along with a host country's discriminatory employment practices? If companies in developed countries shift facilities to developing nations that lack strict environmental and health regulations, or if those companies choose to fill management and other top-level positions in a host nation with people from the home country, whose standards should prevail?

Even the best-informed, best-intentioned executives must rethink their assumptions about business practice in foreign settings. What works in a company's home country can fail in a country with different standards of ethical conduct. Such difficulties are unavoidable for businesspeople who live and work abroad.

But how can managers resolve the problems? What are the principles that can help them work through the maze of cultural differences and establish codes of conduct for globally ethical business practice? How can companies answer the toughest question in global business ethics: What happens when a host country's ethical standards seem lower than the home country's?

Competing Answers

One answer is as old as philosophical discourse. According to cultural relativism, no culture's ethics are better than any other's; therefore there are no international rights and wrongs. If the people of Indonesia tolerate the bribery of their public officials, so what? Their attitude is no better or worse than that of people in Denmark or Singapore who refuse to offer or accept bribes. Likewise, if Belgians fail to find insider trading morally repugnant, who cares? Not enforcing insider-trading laws is no more or less ethical than enforcing such laws.

The cultural relativist's creed—When in Rome, do as the Romans do—is tempting, especially when failing to do as the locals do means forfeiting business opportunities. The inadequacy of cultural relativism, however, becomes apparent when the practices in question are more damaging than petty bribery or insider trading.

In the late 1980s, some European tanneries and pharmaceutical companies were looking for cheap waste-dumping sites. They approached virtually every country on Africa's west coast from Morocco to the Congo. Nigeria agreed to take highly toxic polychlorinated biphenyls. Unprotected local workers, wearing thongs and shorts, unloaded barrels of PCBs and placed them near a residential area. Neither the residents nor the workers knew that the barrels contained toxic waste.

We may denounce governments that permit such abuses, but many countries are unable to police transnational corporations adequately even if they want to. And in many countries, the combination of ineffective enforcement and inadequate regulations leads to behavior by unscrupulous companies that is clearly wrong. A few years ago, for example, a group of investors became interested in restoring the SS *United States*, once a luxurious ocean liner. Before the actual restoration could begin, the ship had to be stripped of its asbestos lining. A bid from a U.S. company, based on U.S. standards for asbestos removal, priced the job at more than $100 million. A company in the Ukranian city of Sevastopol offered to do the work for less than $2 million. In October 1993, the ship was towed to Sevastopol.

Idea in Brief

What should managers working abroad do when they encounter business practices that seem unethical? Should they, in the spirit of cultural relativism, tell themselves to do in Rome as the Romans do? Or should they take an absolutist approach, using the ethical standards they use at home no matter where they are? Many business practices are neither black nor white but exist in a gray zone, a moral free space through which managers must navigate.

Levi Strauss and Motorola have helped managers by treating company values as absolutes and insisting that suppliers and customers do the same. And, perhaps even more important, both companies have developed detailed codes of conduct that provide clear direction on ethical behavior but also leave room for managers to use the moral imagination that will allow them to resolve ethical tensions responsibly and creatively.

A cultural relativist would have no problem with that outcome, but I do. A country has the right to establish its own health and safety regulations, but in the case described above, the standards and the terms of the contract could not possibly have protected workers in Sevastopol from known health risks. Even if the contract met Ukranian standards, ethical businesspeople must object. Cultural relativism is morally blind. There are fundamental values that cross cultures, and companies must uphold them.

At the other end of the spectrum from cultural relativism is ethical imperialism, which directs people to do everywhere exactly as they do at home. Again, an understandably appealing approach but one that is clearly inadequate. Consider the large U.S. computer-products company that in 1993 introduced a course on sexual harassment in its Saudi Arabian facility. Under the banner of global consistency, instructors used the same approach to train Saudi Arabian managers that they had used with U.S. managers: the participants were asked to discuss a case in which a manager makes sexually explicit remarks to a new female employee over drinks in a bar. The instructors failed to consider how the exercise would work in a culture with strict conventions governing relationships between men and women. As a result, the training sessions were ludicrous.

They baffled and offended the Saudi participants, and the message to avoid coercion and sexual discrimination was lost.

The theory behind ethical imperialism is absolutism, which is based on three problematic principles. Absolutists believe that there is a single list of truths, that they can be expressed only with one set of concepts, and that they call for exactly the same behavior around the world.

The first claim clashes with many people's belief that different cultural traditions must be respected. In some cultures, loyalty to a community—family, organization, or society—is the foundation of all ethical behavior. The Japanese, for example, define business ethics in terms of loyalty to their companies, their business networks, and their nation. Americans place a higher value on liberty than on loyalty; the U.S. tradition of rights emphasizes equality, fairness, and individual freedom. It is hard to conclude that truth lies on one side or the other, but an absolutist would have us select just one.

The second problem with absolutism is the presumption that people must express moral truth using only one set of concepts. For instance, some absolutists insist that the language of basic rights provide the framework for any discussion of ethics. That means, though, that entire cultural traditions must be ignored. The notion of a right evolved with the rise of democracy in post-Renaissance Europe and the United States, but the term is not found in either Confucian or Buddhist traditions. We all learn ethics in the context of our particular cultures, and the power in the principles is deeply tied to the way in which they are expressed. Internationally accepted lists of moral principles, such as the United Nations' Universal Declaration of Human Rights, draw on many cultural and religious traditions. As philosopher Michael Walzer has noted, "There is no Esperanto of global ethics."

The third problem with absolutism is the belief in a global standard of ethical behavior. Context must shape ethical practice. Very low wages, for example, may be considered unethical in rich, advanced countries, but developing nations may be acting ethically if they encourage investment and improve living standards by accepting low wages. Likewise, when people are malnourished or starving, a government may be wise to use more fertilizer in order to improve crop yields, even though that means settling for relatively high levels of thermal water pollution.

When cultures have different standards of ethical behavior—and different ways of handling unethical behavior—a company that takes an absolutist approach may find itself making a disastrous mistake. When a manager at a large U.S. specialty-products company in China caught an employee stealing, she followed the company's practice and turned the employee over to the provincial authorities, who executed him. Managers cannot operate in another culture without being aware of that culture's attitudes toward ethics.

If companies can neither adopt a host country's ethics nor extend the home country's standards, what is the answer? Even the traditional litmus test—What would people think of your actions if they were written up on the front page of the newspaper?—is an unreliable guide, for there is no international consensus on standards of business conduct.

Balancing the Extremes: Three Guiding Principles

Companies must help managers distinguish between practices that are merely different and those that are wrong. For relativists, nothing is sacred and nothing is wrong. For absolutists, many things that are different are wrong. Neither extreme illuminates the real world of business decision making. The answer lies somewhere in between.

When it comes to shaping ethical behavior, companies must be guided by three principles.

- Respect for core human values, which determine the absolute moral threshold for all business activities.

- Respect for local traditions.

- The belief that context matters when deciding what is right and what is wrong.

Consider those principles in action. In Japan, people doing business together often exchange gifts—sometimes expensive ones—in keeping with long-standing Japanese tradition. When U.S. and European companies started doing a lot of business in Japan, many Western businesspeople thought that the practice of gift giving might be wrong rather than simply different. To them, accepting a gift felt like accepting a bribe. As Western companies have become more familiar with Japanese traditions, however, most have come to tolerate the practice and to set different limits on gift giving in Japan than they do elsewhere.

Respecting differences is a crucial ethical practice. Research shows that management ethics differ among cultures; respecting those differences means recognizing that some cultures have obvious weaknesses—as well as hidden strengths. Managers in Hong Kong, for example, have a higher tolerance for some forms of bribery than their Western counterparts, but they have a much lower tolerance for the failure to acknowledge a subordinate's work. In some parts of the Far East, stealing credit from a subordinate is nearly an unpardonable sin.

People often equate respect for local traditions with cultural relativism. That is incorrect. Some practices are clearly wrong. Union Carbide's tragic experience in Bhopal, India, provides one example. The company's executives seriously underestimated how much on-site management involvement was needed at the Bhopal plant to compensate for the country's poor infrastructure and regulatory capabilities. In the aftermath of the disastrous gas leak, the lesson is clear: companies using sophisticated technology in a developing country must evaluate that country's ability to oversee its safe use. Since the incident at Bhopal, Union Carbide has become a leader in advising companies on using hazardous technologies safely in developing countries.

Some activities are wrong no matter where they take place. But some practices that are unethical in one setting may be acceptable in another. For instance, the chemical EDB, a soil fungicide, is banned for use in the United States. In hot climates, however, it quickly becomes harmless through exposure to intense solar radiation and high soil temperatures. As long as the chemical is monitored, companies may be able to use EDB ethically in certain parts of the world.

Defining the Ethical Threshold: Core Values

Few ethical questions are easy for managers to answer. But there are some hard truths that must guide managers' actions, a set of what I call *core human values*, which define minimum ethical standards for all companies.[1] The right to good health and the right to economic advancement and an improved standard of living are two core human values. Another is what Westerners call the Golden Rule, which is recognizable in every major religious and ethical tradition around the world. In Book 15 of his *Analects*, for instance, Confucius counsels people to maintain reciprocity, or not to do to others what they do not want done to themselves.

Although no single list would satisfy every scholar, I believe it is possible to articulate three core values that incorporate the work of scores of theologians and philosophers around the world. To be broadly relevant, these values must include elements found in both Western and non-Western cultural and religious traditions. Consider the examples of values in the table "What do these values have in common?"

At first glance, the values expressed in the two lists seem quite different. Nonetheless, in the spirit of what philosopher John Rawls calls *overlapping consensus*, one can see that the seemingly divergent values converge at key points. Despite important differences between Western and non-Western cultural and religious traditions, both express shared attitudes about what it means to be human. First, individuals must not treat others simply as tools; in other words, they must recognize a person's value as a human being. Next, individuals and communities must treat people in ways that respect people's basic rights. Finally, members of a community must work together to support and improve the institutions on which the community depends. I call those three values *respect for human dignity*, *respect for basic rights*, and *good citizenship*.

Those values must be the starting point for all companies as they formulate and evaluate standards of ethical conduct at home and abroad. But they are only a starting point. Companies need much more specific guidelines, and the first step to developing those is to

What do these values have in common?

Non-Western	Western
Kyosei (Japanese): Living and working together for the common good.	Individual liberty
Dharma (Hindu): The fulfillment of inherited duty.	Egalitarianism
Santutthi (Buddhist): The importance of limited desires.	Political participation
Zakat (Muslim): The duty to give alms to the Muslim poor.	Human rights

translate the core human values into core values for business. What does it mean, for example, for a company to respect human dignity? How can a company be a good citizen?

I believe that companies can respect human dignity by creating and sustaining a corporate culture in which employees, customers, and suppliers are treated not as means to an end but as people whose intrinsic value must be acknowledged, and by producing safe products and services in a safe workplace. Companies can respect basic rights by acting in ways that support and protect the individual rights of employees, customers, and surrounding communities, and by avoiding relationships that violate human beings' rights to health, education, safety, and an adequate standard of living. And companies can be good citizens by supporting essential social institutions, such as the economic system and the education system, and by working with host governments and other organizations to protect the environment.

The core values establish a moral compass for business practice. They can help companies identify practices that are acceptable and those that are intolerable—even if the practices are compatible with a host country's norms and laws. Dumping pollutants near people's homes and accepting inadequate standards for handling hazardous materials are two examples of actions that violate core values.

Similarly, if employing children prevents them from receiving a basic education, the practice is intolerable. Lying about product specifications in the act of selling may not affect human lives directly, but it too is intolerable because it violates the trust that is needed to sustain a corporate culture in which customers are respected.

Sometimes it is not a company's actions but those of a supplier or customer that pose problems. Take the case of the Tan family, a large supplier for Levi Strauss. The Tans were allegedly forcing 1,200 Chinese and Filipino women to work 74 hours per week in guarded compounds on the Mariana Islands. In 1992, after repeated warnings to the Tans, Levi Strauss broke off business relations with them.

Creating an Ethical Corporate Culture

The core values for business that I have enumerated can help companies begin to exercise ethical judgment and think about how to operate ethically in foreign cultures, but they are not specific enough to guide managers through actual ethical dilemmas. Levi Strauss relied on a written code of conduct when figuring out how to deal with the Tan family. The company's Global Sourcing and Operating Guidelines, formerly called the Business Partner Terms of Engagement, state that Levi Strauss will "seek to identify and utilize business partners who aspire as individuals and in the conduct of all their businesses to a set of ethical standards not incompatible with our own." Whenever intolerable business situations arise, managers should be guided by precise statements that spell out the behavior and operating practices that the company demands.

Ninety percent of all *Fortune* 500 companies have codes of conduct, and 70% have statements of vision and values. In Europe and the Far East, the percentages are lower but are increasing rapidly. Does that mean that most companies have what they need? Hardly. Even though most large U.S. companies have both statements of values and codes of conduct, many might be better off if they didn't. Too many companies don't do anything with the documents; they simply paste them on the wall to impress employees, customers, suppliers, and the public. As a result, the senior managers who drafted the statements lose credibility by proclaiming values and not living up to them. Companies such as Johnson & Johnson, Levi Strauss, Motorola, Texas Instruments, and Lockheed Martin, however, do a great deal to make the words meaningful. Johnson & Johnson, for example, has become well known for its Credo Challenge sessions, in which managers discuss ethics in the context of their current business problems and are invited to criticize the company's credo and make suggestions for changes. The participants' ideas are passed on to the company's senior managers. Lockheed Martin has created an innovative site on the World Wide Web and on its local network that gives employees, customers, and suppliers access to the company's ethical code and the chance to voice complaints.

Codes of conduct must provide clear direction about ethical behavior when the temptation to behave unethically is strongest. The pronouncement in a code of conduct that bribery is unacceptable is useless unless accompanied by guidelines for gift giving, payments to get goods through customs, and "requests" from intermediaries who are hired to ask for bribes.

Motorola's values are stated very simply as "How we will always act: [with] constant respect for people [and] uncompromising integrity." The company's code of conduct, however, is explicit about actual business practice. With respect to bribery, for example, the code states that the "funds and assets of Motorola shall not be used, directly or indirectly, for illegal payments of any kind." It is unambiguous about what sort of payment is illegal: "the payment of a bribe to a public official or the kickback of funds to an employee of a customer...." The code goes on to prescribe specific procedures for handling commissions to intermediaries, issuing sales invoices, and disclosing confidential information in a sales transaction—all situations in which employees might have an opportunity to accept or offer bribes.

Codes of conduct must be explicit to be useful, but they must also leave room for a manager to use his or her judgment in situations requiring cultural sensitivity. Host-country employees shouldn't be forced to adopt all home-country values and renounce their own. Again, Motorola's code is exemplary. First, it gives clear direction: "Employees of Motorola will respect the laws, customs, and traditions of each country in which they operate, but will, at the same time, engage in no course of conduct which, even if legal, customary, and accepted in any such country, could be deemed to be in violation of the accepted business ethics of Motorola or the laws of the United States relating to business ethics." After laying down such absolutes, Motorola's code then makes clear when individual judgment will be necessary. For example, employees may sometimes accept certain kinds of small gifts "in rare circumstances, where the refusal to accept a gift" would injure Motorola's "legitimate business interests." Under certain circumstances, such gifts "may be accepted so long as the gift inures to the benefit of Motorola" and not "to the benefit of the Motorola employee."

Striking the appropriate balance between providing clear direction and leaving room for individual judgment makes crafting corporate values statements and ethics codes one of the hardest tasks that executives confront. The words are only a start. A company's leaders need to refer often to their organization's credo and code and must themselves be credible, committed, and consistent. If senior managers act as though ethics don't matter, the rest of the company's employees won't think they do, either.

Conflicts of Development and Conflicts of Tradition

Managers living and working abroad who are not prepared to grapple with moral ambiguity and tension should pack their bags and come home. The view that all business practices can be categorized as either ethical or unethical is too simple. As Einstein is reported to have said, "Things should be as simple as possible—but no simpler." Many business practices that are considered unethical in one setting may be ethical in another. Such activities are neither black nor white but exist in what Thomas Dunfee and I have called *moral free space*.[2] In this gray zone, there are no tight prescriptions for a company's behavior. Managers must chart their own courses—as long as they do not violate core human values.

Consider the following example. Some successful Indian companies offer employees the opportunity for one of their children to gain a job with the company once the child has completed a certain level in school. The companies honor this commitment even when other applicants are more qualified than an employee's child. The perk is extremely valuable in a country where jobs are hard to find, and it reflects the Indian culture's belief that the West has gone too far in allowing economic opportunities to break up families. Not surprisingly, the perk is among the most cherished by employees, but in most Western countries, it would be branded unacceptable nepotism. In the United States, for example, the ethical principle of equal opportunity holds that jobs should go to the applicants with the best qualifications. If a U.S. company made such promises to its employees, it would violate regulations established by the Equal Employment Opportunity Commission. Given this difference in ethical attitudes, how should U.S. managers react to Indian nepotism? Should they condemn the Indian companies, refusing to accept them as partners or suppliers until they agree to clean up their act?

Despite the obvious tension between nepotism and principles of equal opportunity, I cannot condemn the practice for Indians. In a country, such as India, that emphasizes clan and family relationships and has catastrophic levels of unemployment, the practice must be viewed in moral free space. The decision to allow a special perk for employees and their children is not necessarily wrong—at least for members of that country.

How can managers discover the limits of moral free space? That is, how can they learn to distinguish a value in tension with their own from one that is intolerable? Helping managers develop good ethical judgment requires companies to be clear about their core values and codes of conduct. But even the most explicit set of guidelines cannot always provide answers. That is especially true in the thorniest ethical dilemmas, in which the host country's ethical standards not only are different but also seem lower than the home country's. Managers must recognize that when countries have different ethical standards, there are two types of conflict that commonly arise. Each type requires its own line of reasoning.

In the first type of conflict, which I call a *conflict of relative development*, ethical standards conflict because of the countries' different levels of economic development. As mentioned before, developing countries may accept wage rates that seem inhumane to more advanced countries in order to attract investment. As economic conditions in a developing country improve, the incidence of that sort of conflict usually decreases. The second type of conflict is a *conflict of cultural tradition*. For example, Saudi Arabia, unlike most other countries, does not allow women to serve as corporate managers. Instead, women may work in only a few professions, such as education and health care. The prohibition stems from strongly held religious and cultural beliefs; any increase in the country's level of economic development, which is already quite high, is not likely to change the rules.

To resolve a conflict of relative development, a manager must ask the following question: Would the practice be acceptable at home if my country were in a similar stage of economic development? Consider the difference between wage and safety standards in the United States and in Angola, where citizens accept lower standards on both counts. If a U.S. oil company is hiring Angolans to work on an offshore Angolan oil rig, can the company pay them lower wages than it pays U.S. workers in the Gulf of Mexico? Reasonable people have to answer yes if the alternative for Angola is the loss of both the foreign investment and the jobs.

Consider, too, differences in regulatory environments. In the 1980s, the government of India fought hard to be able to import Ciba-Geigy's Entero Vioform, a drug known to be enormously effective in fighting dysentery but one that had been banned in the United States because some users experienced side effects. Although dysentery was not a big problem in the United States, in India, poor public sanitation was contributing to epidemic levels of the disease. Was it unethical to make the drug available in India after it had been banned in the United States? On the contrary, rational people should consider it unethical not to do so. Apply our test: Would the United States, at an earlier stage of development, have used this drug despite its side effects? The answer is clearly yes.

But there are many instances when the answer to similar questions is no. Sometimes a host country's standards are inadequate at any level of economic development. If a country's pollution standards are so low that working on an oil rig would considerably increase a person's risk of developing cancer, foreign oil companies must refuse to do business there. Likewise, if the dangerous side effects of a drug treatment outweigh its benefits, managers should not accept health standards that ignore the risks.

When relative economic conditions do not drive tensions, there is a more objective test for resolving ethical problems. Managers should deem a practice permissible only if they can answer no to both of the following questions: Is it possible to conduct business successfully in the host country without undertaking the practice? and Is the practice a violation of a core human value? Japanese gift giving is a perfect example of a conflict of cultural tradition. Most experienced businesspeople, Japanese and non-Japanese alike, would agree that doing business in Japan would be virtually impossible without adopting the practice. Does gift giving violate a core human value? I cannot identify one that it violates. As a result, gift giving may be permissible for foreign companies in Japan even if it conflicts with ethical attitudes at home. In fact, that conclusion is widely accepted, even by companies such as Texas Instruments and IBM, which are outspoken against bribery.

Does it follow that all nonmonetary gifts are acceptable or that bribes are generally acceptable in countries where they are common? Not at all. (See the sidebar "The Problem with Bribery.") What makes the routine practice of gift giving acceptable in Japan are the limits in its scope and intention. When gift giving moves outside those limits, it soon collides with core human values. For example, when Carl Kotchian, president of Lockheed in the 1970s, carried suitcases full of cash to Japanese politicians, he went beyond the norms established by Japanese tradition. That incident galvanized opinion in the United States Congress and helped lead to passage of the Foreign Corrupt Practices Act. Likewise, Roh Tae Woo went beyond the norms established by Korean cultural tradition when he accepted $635.4 million in bribes as president of the Republic of Korea between 1988 and 1993.

The Problem with Bribery

BRIBERY IS WIDESPREAD AND INSIDIOUS. Managers in transnational companies routinely confront bribery even though most countries have laws against it. The fact is that officials in many developing countries wink at the practice, and the salaries of local bureaucrats are so low that many consider bribes a form of remuneration. The U.S. Foreign Corrupt Practices Act defines allowable limits on petty bribery in the form of routine payments required to move goods through customs. But demands for bribes often exceed those limits, and there is seldom a good solution.

Bribery disrupts distribution channels when goods languish on docks until local handlers are paid off, and it destroys incentives to compete on quality and cost when purchasing decisions are based on who pays what under the table. Refusing to acquiesce is often tantamount to giving business to unscrupulous companies.

I believe that even routine bribery is intolerable. Bribery undermines market efficiency and predictability, thus ultimately denying people their right to a minimal standard of living. Some degree of ethical commitment—some sense that everyone will play by the rules—is necessary for a sound economy. Without an ability to predict outcomes, who would be willing to invest?

There was a U.S. company whose shipping crates were regularly pilfered by handlers on the docks of Rio de Janeiro. The handlers would take about 10% of the contents of the crates, but the company was never sure which 10% it would be. In a partial solution, the company began sending two crates—the first with 90% of the merchandise, the second with 10%. The handlers learned to take the second crate and leave the first untouched. From the company's perspective, at least knowing which goods it would lose was an improvement.

Bribery does more than destroy predictability; it undermines essential social and economic systems. That truth is not lost on businesspeople in countries where the practice is woven into the social fabric. CEOs in India admit that their companies engage constantly in bribery, and they say that they have considerable disgust for the practice. They blame government policies in part, but Indian executives also know that their country's business practices perpetuate corrupt behavior. Anyone walking the streets of Calcutta, where it is clear that even a dramatic redistribution of wealth would still leave most of India's inhabitants in dire poverty, comes face-to-face with the devastating effects of corruption.

Guidelines for Ethical Leadership

Learning to spot intolerable practices and to exercise good judgment when ethical conflicts arise requires practice. Creating a company culture that rewards ethical behavior is essential. The following guidelines for developing a global ethical perspective among managers can help.

Treat corporate values and formal standards of conduct as absolutes

Whatever ethical standards a company chooses, it cannot waver on its principles either at home or abroad. Consider what has become part of company lore at Motorola. Around 1950, a senior executive was negotiating with officials of a South American government on a $10 million sale that would have increased the company's annual net profits by nearly 25%. As the negotiations neared completion, however, the executive walked away from the deal because the officials were asking for $1 million for "fees." CEO Robert Galvin not only supported the executive's decision but also made it clear that Motorola would neither accept the sale on any terms nor do business with those government officials again. Retold over the decades, this story demonstrating Galvin's resolve has helped cement a culture of ethics for thousands of employees at Motorola.

Design and implement conditions of engagement for suppliers and customers

Will your company do business with any customer or supplier? What if a customer or supplier uses child labor? What if it has strong links with organized crime? What if it pressures your company to break a host country's laws? Such issues are best not left for spur-of-the-moment decisions. Some companies have realized that. Sears, for instance, has developed a policy of not contracting production to companies that use prison labor or infringe on workers' rights to health and safety. And BankAmerica has specified as a condition for many of its loans to developing countries that environmental standards and human rights must be observed.

Allow foreign business units to help formulate ethical standards and interpret ethical issues

The French pharmaceutical company Rhône-Poulenc Rorer has allowed foreign subsidiaries to augment lists of corporate ethical principles with their own suggestions. Texas Instruments has paid special attention to issues of international business ethics by creating the Global Business Practices Council, which is made up of managers from countries in which the company operates. With the overarching intent to create a "global ethics strategy, locally deployed," the council's mandate is to provide ethics education and create local processes that will help managers in the company's foreign business units resolve ethical conflicts.

In host countries, support efforts to decrease institutional corruption

Individual managers will not be able to wipe out corruption in a host country, no matter how many bribes they turn down. When a host country's tax system, import and export procedures, and procurement practices favor unethical players, companies must take action.

Many companies have begun to participate in reforming host-country institutions. General Electric, for example, has taken a strong stand in India, using the media to make repeated condemnations of bribery in business and government. General Electric and others have found, however, that a single company usually cannot drive out entrenched corruption. Transparency International, an organization based in Germany, has been effective in helping coalitions of companies, government officials, and others work to reform bribery-ridden bureaucracies in Russia, Bangladesh, and elsewhere.

Exercise moral imagination

Using moral imagination means resolving tensions responsibly and creatively. Coca-Cola, for instance, has consistently turned down requests for bribes from Egyptian officials but has managed to gain political support and public trust by sponsoring a project to plant fruit trees. And take the example of Levi Strauss, which discovered in the early 1990s that two of its suppliers in Bangladesh were employing children under the age of 14—a practice that violated the company's principles but was tolerated in Bangladesh. Forcing the suppliers to fire the children would not have ensured that the children received an education, and it would have caused serious hardship for the families depending on the children's wages. In a creative arrangement, the suppliers agreed to pay the children's regular wages while they attended school and to offer each child a job at age 14. Levi Strauss, in turn, agreed to pay the children's tuition and provide books and uniforms. That arrangement allowed Levi Strauss to uphold its principles and provide long-term benefits to its host country.

Many people think of values as soft; to some they are usually unspoken. A South Seas island society uses the word *mokita*, which means, "the truth that everybody knows but nobody speaks." However difficult they are to articulate, values affect how we all behave. In a global business environment, values in tension are the rule rather than the exception. Without a company's commitment, statements of values and codes of ethics end up as empty platitudes that provide managers with no foundation for behaving ethically. Employees need and deserve more, and responsible members of the global business community can set examples for others to follow. The dark consequences of incidents such as Union Carbide's disaster in Bhopal remind us how high the stakes can be.

Originally published in September–October 1996. Reprint 96502

Notes

1. In other writings, Thomas W. Dunfee and I have used the term *hypernorm* instead of *core human value*.
2. Thomas Donaldson and Thomas W. Dunfee, "Toward a Unified Conception of Business Ethics: Integrative Social Contracts Theory," *Academy of Management Review*, April 1994; and "Integrative Social Contracts Theory: A Communitarian Conception of Economic Ethics," *Economics and Philosophy*, spring 1995.

Global Business Speaks English

by Tsedal Neeley

READY OR NOT, English is now the global language of business. More and more multinational companies are mandating English as the common corporate language—Airbus, Daimler-Chrysler, Fast Retailing, Nokia, Renault, Samsung, SAP, Technicolor, and Microsoft in Beijing, to name a few—in an attempt to facilitate communication and performance across geographically diverse functions and business endeavors.

Adopting a common mode of speech isn't just a good idea; it's a must, even for an American company with operations overseas, for instance, or a French company focused on domestic customers. Imagine that a group of salespeople from a company's Paris headquarters get together for a meeting. Why would you care whether they all could speak English? Now consider that the same group goes on a sales call to a company also based in Paris, not realizing that the potential customer would be bringing in employees from other locations who didn't speak French. This happened at one company I worked with. Sitting together in Paris, employees of those two French companies couldn't close a deal because the people in the room couldn't communicate. It was a shocking wake-up call, and the company soon adopted an English corporate language strategy.

Similar concerns drove Hiroshi Mikitani, the CEO of Rakuten—Japan's largest online marketplace—to mandate in March 2010 that

English would be the company's official language of business. The company's goal was to become the number one internet services company in the world, and Mikitani believed that the new policy—which would affect some 7,100 Japanese employees—was vital to achieving that end, especially as expansion plans were concentrated outside Japan. He also felt responsible for contributing to an expanded worldview for his country, a conservative island nation.

The multibillion-dollar company—a cross between Amazon.com and eBay—was on a growth spree: It had acquired PriceMinister.com in France, Buy.com and FreeCause in the U.S., Play.com in the UK, Tradoria in Germany, Kobo eBooks in Canada, and established joint ventures with major companies in China, Indonesia, Taiwan, Thailand, and Brazil. Serious about the language change, Mikitani announced the plan to employees not in Japanese but in English. Overnight, the Japanese language cafeteria menus were replaced, as were elevator directories. And he stated that employees would have to demonstrate competence on an international English scoring system within two years—or risk demotion or even dismissal.

The media instantly picked up the story, and corporate Japan reacted with fascination and disdain. Honda's CEO, Takanobu Ito, publicly asserted, "It's stupid for a Japanese company to only use English in Japan when the workforce is mainly Japanese." But Mikitani was confident that it was the right move, and the policy is bearing fruit. The English mandate has allowed Mikitani to create a remarkably diverse and powerful organization. Today, three out of six senior executives in his engineering organization aren't Japanese; they don't even speak Japanese. The company continues to aggressively seek the best talent from around the globe. Half of Rakuten's Japanese employees now can adequately engage in internal communication in English, and 25% communicate in English with partners and coworkers in foreign subsidiaries on a regular basis.

Adopting a global language policy is not easy, and companies invariably stumble along the way. It's radical, and it's almost certain to meet with staunch resistance from employees. Many may feel at a disadvantage if their English isn't as good as others', team dynamics and performance can suffer, and national pride can get in the way.

Idea in Brief

Companies are increasingly adopting English as the common corporate language, no matter where they're based. Unrestricted multilingualism is inefficient and gets in the way of accomplishing business goals. If people can't communicate effectively, sales get lost, merger integration drags, productivity slows, and so on. Single-language policies help companies avoid these problems, and English is the natural choice because it is already the dominant language of business.

Implementing an English-only policy is difficult and messy.

People may view it as an affront to their cultural identity, or fear that they won't be able to learn enough English to keep up.

However, there's a lot that companies can do to help people along—including providing training, modeling the right behaviors themselves, and keeping the reasons for change front and center at all times.

And in fact, the challenge of getting up to speed may be less daunting than people think. You don't have to reach native fluency to be effective at work. For most people, 3,000 to 5,000 words will do it.

But to survive and thrive in a global economy, companies must overcome language barriers—and English will almost always be the common ground, at least for now.

The fastest-spreading language in human history, English is spoken at a useful level by some 1.75 billion people worldwide—that's one in every four of us. There are close to 385 million native speakers in countries like the U.S. and Australia, about a billion fluent speakers in formerly colonized nations such as India and Nigeria, and millions of people around the world who've studied it as a second language. An estimated 565 million people use it on the internet.

The benefits of "Englishnization," as Mikitani calls it, are significant; however, relatively few companies have systematically implemented an English-language policy with sustained results. Through my research and work over the past decade with companies, I've developed an adoption framework to guide companies in their language efforts. There's still a lot to learn, but success stories do exist. Adopters will find significant advantages.

Why English Only?

There's no question that unrestricted multilingualism is inefficient and can prevent important interactions from taking place and get in the way of achieving key goals. The need to tightly coordinate tasks and work with customers and partners worldwide has accelerated the move toward English as the official language of business no matter where companies are headquartered.

Three primary reasons are driving the move toward English as a corporate standard.

Competitive pressure

If you want to buy or sell, you have to be able to communicate with a diverse range of customers, suppliers, and other business partners. If you're lucky, they'll share your native language—but you can't count on it. Companies that fail to devise a language strategy are essentially limiting their growth opportunities to the markets where their language is spoken, clearly putting themselves at a disadvantage to competitors that have adopted English-only policies.

Globalization of tasks and resources

Language differences can cause a bottleneck—a Tower of Babel, as it were—when geographically dispersed employees have to work together to meet corporate goals. An employee from Belgium may need input from an enterprise in Beirut or Mexico. Without common ground, communication will suffer. Better language comprehension gives employees more firsthand information, which is vital to good decision making. Swiss food giant Nestlé saw great efficiency improvements in purchasing and hiring thanks to its enforcement of English as a company standard.

M&A integration across national boundaries

Negotiations regarding a merger or acquisition are complicated enough when everybody speaks the same language. But when they don't, nuances are easily lost, even in simple e-mail exchanges. Also,

Will Mandarin Be Next?

GIVEN THE SIZE AND GROWTH of the Chinese economy, why move to an English-only policy? Isn't it possible that Mandarin could overtake English as the global language of business? It's possible, but unlikely. There are two reasons for this.

First, English has a giant head start. China can't replicate Britain's colonial history. The British Empire began embedding the English language in many parts of the world as early as the 16th century. Philanthropic work by American and British organizations further spread English, long before corporations began to adopt it at the workplace.

Second, for much of the world, Mandarin is extremely difficult to learn. It's easier to pick up "broken English" than "broken Mandarin." Knowing Mandarin—or any language spoken by huge numbers of people—is an advantage, clearly. But for now, Mandarin is not a realistic option for a one-language policy.

cross-cultural integration is notoriously tricky; that's why when Germany's Hoechst and France's Rhône-Poulenc merged in 1998 to create Aventis, the fifth largest worldwide pharmaceutical company, the new firm chose English as its operating language over French or German to avoid playing favorites. A branding element can also come into play. In the 1990s, a relatively unknown, midsize Italian appliance maker, Merloni, adopted English to further its international image, which gave it an edge when acquiring Russian and British companies.

Obstacles to Successful English-Language Policies

To be sure, one-language policies can have repercussions that decrease efficiency. Evidence from my research at Rakuten—along with a study I conducted with Pamela Hinds of Stanford University and Catherine Cramton of George Mason University at a company I'll call GlobalTech and a study I conducted at a firm I'll call FrenchCo— reveals costs that global English-language rules can create. Proper rollout mitigates the risks, but even well-considered plans can encounter pitfalls. Here are some of the most common.

Change always comes as a shock

No amount of warning and preparation can entirely prevent the psychological blow to employees when proposed change becomes reality. When Marie (all names in this article are disguised, with the exception of Mikitani and Ito) first learned of FrenchCo's English-only policy, she was excited. She had been communicating in English with non-French partners for some time, and she saw the proposed policy as a positive sign that the company was becoming more international. That is, until she attended a routine meeting that was normally held in French. "I didn't realize that the very first meeting after the rule came out was really going to be in English. It was a shock," Marie says. She recalls walking into the meeting with a lot of energy—until she noticed the translator headsets.

"They're humiliating," she says. "I felt like an observer rather than a participant at my own company."

Compliance is spotty

An English mandate created a different problem for a service representative at GlobalTech. Based in Germany, the technology firm had subsidiaries worldwide. Hans, a service representative, received a frantic call from his boss when a key customer's multimillion-dollar financial services operation ground to a halt as a result of a software glitch. Hundreds of thousands of dollars were at stake for both the customer and GlobalTech. Hans quickly placed a call to the technical department in India, but the software team was unable to jump on the problem because all communications about it were in German—despite the English-only policy instituted two years earlier requiring that all internal communications (meetings, e-mails, documents, and phone calls) be carried out in English. As Hans waited for documents to be translated, the crisis continued to escalate. Two years into the implementation, adoption was dragging.

Self-confidence erodes

When nonnative speakers are forced to communicate in English, they can feel that their worth to the company has been diminished, regardless of their fluency level. "The most difficult thing is to have to admit that one's value as an English speaker overshadows one's real value," a FrenchCo employee says. "For the past 30 years the company did not ask us to develop our foreign-language skills or offer us the opportunity to do so," he points out. "Now, it is difficult to accept the fact that we are disqualified." Employees facing one-language policies often worry that the best jobs will be offered only to those with strong English skills, regardless of content expertise.

When my colleagues and I interviewed 164 employees at GlobalTech two years after the company's English-only policy had been implemented, we found that nearly 70% of employees continued to experience frustration with it. At FrenchCo, 56% of medium-fluency English speakers and 42% of low-fluency speakers reported worrying about job advancement because of their relatively limited English skills. Such feelings are common when companies merely announce the new policy and offer language classes rather than implement the shift in a systematic way. It's worth noting that employees often underestimate their own abilities or overestimate the challenge of developing sufficient fluency. (See the exhibit "Gauging fluency.")

Gauging fluency

Progressing from beginner level to advanced—which greatly improves an employee's ability to communicate—involves mastering around 3,500 words. That's a far less daunting task than adding the 10,000 words necessary to move from advanced to native speaker, for which the payoff may be lower.

1,500	3,000	5,000	15,000 words
Beginner	**Intermediate**	**Advanced**	**Native speakers**
These employees are able to cope with basic situations.	At this level, employees can function productively in business settings. They can understand verbal and written communications and express themselves; however, fine shades of meaning may escape them.	These speakers are comfortable with technical terms and nuanced discussion. They may begin to experience diminishing returns on their language efforts.	These employees speak fluently and idiomatically and have all means at their disposal to communicate effectively.

Job security falters

Even though achieving sufficient fluency is possible for most, the reality is that with adoption of an English-only policy, employees' job requirements change—sometimes overnight. That can be a bitter pill to swallow, especially among top performers. Rakuten's Mikitani didn't mince words with his employees: He was clear that he would demote people who didn't develop their English proficiency.

Employees resist

It's not unusual to hear nonnative speakers revert to their own language at the expense of their English-speaking colleagues, often because it's faster and easier to conduct meetings in their mother tongue. Others may take more aggressive measures to avoid speaking English, such as holding meetings at inopportune times. Employees in Asia might schedule a global meeting that falls during the middle of the night in England, for instance. In doing so, nonnative speakers shift their anxiety and loss of power to native speakers.

Many FrenchCo employees said that when they felt that their relatively poor language skills could become conspicuous and have career-related consequences, they simply stopped contributing to common discourse. "They're afraid to make mistakes," an HR manager at the firm explains, "so they will just not speak at all."

In other cases, documents that are supposed to be composed in English may be written in the mother tongue—as experienced by Hans at GlobalTech—or not written at all. "It's too hard to write in English, so I don't do it!" one GlobalTech employee notes. "And then there's no documentation at all."

Performance suffers

The bottom line takes a hit when employees stop participating in group settings. Once participation ebbs, processes fall apart. Companies miss out on new ideas that might have been generated in meetings. People don't report costly errors or offer observations about mistakes or questionable decisions. One of the engineers at GlobalTech's Indian office explained that when meetings reverted into German his ability to contribute was cut off. He lost important

Implementation Tips

EVEN WHEN LANGUAGE MANDATES are implemented with care and forethought, negative emotional and organizational dynamics can still arise. But their power to derail careers and company work can be significantly mitigated by adequately preparing people and systems for the change. Here are steps that companies can take to manage English-only policies.

1. Involve All Employees

Before a company introduces a global English policy, leaders should make a persuasive case for why it matters to employees and the organization. Employees must be assured that they will be supported in building their language skills. Companywide cultural-awareness training will help nonnative speakers feel heard and valued. Leaders should rally workers behind using English to accomplish goals, rather than learn it to meet proficiency standards.

2. Managers Are Referees and Enforcers

Managers must take responsibility for ensuring compliance, and they'll need training in how to productively address sensitive issues arising from the radical change. Groups should set norms prescribing how members will interact, and managers should monitor behavior accordingly. For instance, managers should correct employees who switch into their mother tongue.

3. Native Speakers Must Level the Playing Field

Native speakers can learn to speak more slowly and simplify their vocabularies. They should refrain from dominating conversations and encourage nonnative speakers to contribute. Native speakers may need coaching on how to bring along less proficient colleagues who are working at a disadvantage.

4. Nonnative Speakers Must Comply

Nonnative speakers have a responsibility to comply with the global English policy and to refrain from reverting to their mother tongue, even in informal meetings or communications. More-aggressive actions that exclude or ostracize native speakers, such as scheduling meetings at inopportune times, should be strongly discouraged.

---

information—particularly in side exchanges—despite receiving meeting notes afterward. Often those quick asides contained important contextual information, background analyses, or hypotheses about the root cause of a particular problem. He neither participated in the meetings nor learned from the problem-solving discussions.

An Adoption Framework

Converting the primary language of a business is no small task. In my work I've developed a framework for assessing readiness and guidelines for adopting the shift. Adoption depends on two key factors: employee buy-in and belief in capacity. Buy-in is the degree to which employees believe that a single language will produce benefits for them or the organization. Belief in their own capacity is the extent to which they are confident that they can gain enough fluency to pass muster.

The two dimensions combine to produce four categories of response to the change, as shown in the exhibit "Four types of employee response." Ideally, employees would fall in what I call the "inspired" category—those who are excited about the move and confident that they can make the shift. They're optimistic and likely to embrace the challenge. But undoubtedly, some employees will feel "oppressed." Those people don't think the change is a good idea, and they don't think they'll cut it.

Four types of employee response

	Frustrated	Inspired
Strong buy-in	"My company and I would benefit if I learned English, but I don't think I can do it."	"I am capable of learning English, and it would be good for me and my company if I did."
Weak buy-in	**Oppressed** "I don't think I'm capable of learning English, and I don't see the benefit to me or my company to learn it."	**Indifferent** "I can learn English, but I don't see the benefit for me or my company."

Do I believe that it is a good idea?

Low belief — High belief

Can I do this?

The reality is that without buy-in, employees won't bother to brush up their language; without belief, they'll lose hope. I've identified some guidelines managers can follow to help people along. Rakuten's Mikitani has successfully implemented a version of this framework.

Leaders and managers can help employees move from one box to another more easily than you might expect. There are fairly simple strategies that aid the shift, typically involving some combination of a strong psychological boost and practical training. To shift employees from "frustrated" to "inspired," for instance, managers must offer constant encouragement and an array of language-development opportunities. To shift employees from "indifferent" to "inspired," managers must work on improving buy-in—once these employees feel invested in the change, their skills will follow.

Improving belief in capacity

Managers can use four strategies to help people boost their belief in their ability to develop language proficiency.

Offer opportunities to gain experience with language. Whether through education, employment, or living abroad, experience tends to give people the confidence they need to succeed in this task. You can't change past experience, but you can provide opportunities, such as overseas language training and job rotations, that open new doors and allow employees to stretch their skills. Rakuten has sent senior executives to English-speaking Countries like the UK and the U.S. for full language immersion training. Employees have also been offered weeklong language-training programs in the Philippines. Although not easily scalable to 7,100 Japanese employees, the programs successfully produced individuals with functional English skills. Rakuten also plans to send more than 1,000 engineers to technology conferences outside Japan.

Foster positive attitudes. Attitudes are contagious: People's faith in their own capabilities grows when they see others around them—peers, managers, friends—having positive experiences with the radical change. The reverse is also true, unfortunately. Managers can model good risk-taking behaviors by showing that they too are trying new things, making mistakes, and learning from those mistakes.

Mikitani focused his personal attention on middle managers because he knew that collectively they could influence thousands of employees. He encouraged them to constantly improve their own language skills and even offered to teach them English himself if need be. (Nobody took him up on the offer.) He also encouraged managers to support their subordinates in their efforts to develop their language proficiency.

Use verbal persuasion. Encouragement and positive reinforcement from managers and executives—simple statements like "You can do it" or "I believe in you"—make all the difference. To mitigate turnover threats at Rakuten, managers identified talent that the company wanted to retain and tailored special programs for them, all the while cheering them on. Also, Mikitani repeatedly assured his entire workforce that he would do everything in his power to help every employee meet his or her English-proficiency goals. He made it clear that he believes that with effort everyone can adequately learn the language of business and that he did not want to see anyone leave the company because of the English-only policy.

Encourage good study habits. Companies need to contract with language vendors who specialize in helping employees at various levels of proficiency. The vendors need to be intimately familiar with the company context so that they can guide employees' learning, from how best to allocate their time in improving skills to strategies for composing e-mails in English. Rakuten considers language development to be part of every job and grants people time during the workday to devote to it. Every morning, employees can be seen flipping through their study books in the company's cafeteria or navigating their e-learning portals.

What About Cultural Identity?

MANY GLOBAL EMPLOYEES fear that an English-only policy will strip them of their cultural heritage. I propose an alternative point of view. The more people you can communicate with, the better positioned you are to spread your culture and your message. If people can't understand what you're saying, they can't engage with your company or your brand.

Improving employee buy-in

Shifts in buy-in call for different measures. But they don't operate in isolation: Buy-in and belief go together. Strategies that can help people feel more confident include:

Messaging, messaging, and more messaging. Continual communication from the CEO, executives, and managers is critical. Leaders should stress the importance of globalization in achieving the company's mission and strategy and demonstrate how language supports that. At Rakuten, Mikitani signaled the importance of the English-language policy to his entire organization relentlessly. For instance, each week some 120 managers would submit their business reports, and he would reply to each of them pushing them to develop their language skills. I surveyed employees before and after Rakuten implemented the adoption framework. Results indicated a dramatic increase in buy-in after Mikitani showed his employees that he was "obsessed and committed to Englishnization," as he put it. The vast majority of the employees surveyed said that the policy was a "necessary" move.

Internal marketing. Because a language transformation is a multiyear process whose complexity far exceeds most other change efforts, it is crucial to maintain employee buy-in over time. At Rakuten, the now-English intranet regularly features employee success stories with emphasis on best practices for increasing language competence. Companywide meetings are also held monthly to discuss the English-language policy.

Branding. Managers should encourage people to self-identify as global rather than local employees. It's difficult to develop a global identity with limited exposure to an international environment, of course. Rakuten tackled this challenge by instituting an enterprise-wide social network to promote cross-national interactions. Employees now interact and engage with colleagues worldwide through the company's social networking site.

Adopting a universal English policy is not the end of leadership challenges posed by global communication. Using English as a business language can damage employee morale, create unhealthy divides between native and nonnative speakers, and decrease the overall productivity of team members. Leaders must avoid and soften these potential pitfalls by building an environment in which employees can embrace a global English policy with relative ease. In this way, companies can improve communication and collaboration.

When I asked Mikitani what advice he'd give other CEOs when it comes to enforcing a one-language mandate, he was emphatic about discipline. CEOs need to be role models: If they don't stick to the program, nobody else will. Mikitani even holds one-on-one performance reviews with his top Japanese executives in English. "If you forgive a little," he says, "you'll give up everything."

Mikitani doesn't fear resistance. He believes, as I do, that you can counteract it—and ultimately bring about significant transformation in employees' beliefs and buy-in. A global language change takes perseverance and time, but if you want to surpass your rivals, it's no longer a matter of choice.

Originally published in May 2012. Reprint R1205H

10 Rules for Managing Global Innovation

by Keeley Wilson and Yves L. Doz

COMPANIES ARE WELL AWARE that hidden in their dispersed, global operations is a treasure trove of ideas and capabilities for innovation. But it's proving harder than expected to unearth those ideas or exploit those capabilities in global innovation projects. Some of the challenges of global projects are familiar: figuring out the right role for top executives, for example, or finding a good balance between formal and informal project management processes.

But although the challenges may be familiar, the solutions are not; what works for an innovation project conducted in a single location doesn't necessarily work for one dispersed across many sites around the world. That's partly because many important enablers of innovation happen naturally in colocation. Single location projects draw on large reservoirs of shared tacit knowledge and trust, and when issues arise, senior management is on hand to make decisions and provide direction and support. Team members share the same language, culture, and norms, enabling flexibility and iterative learning as the project unfolds.

When a project spans multiple locations, many of those natural benefits—often taken for granted—are lost. Part of the challenge of dispersed innovation thus becomes how to replicate the positive aspects of colocation while harnessing the unique benefits of a global initiative. To explore this challenge, we spent more than a decade doing field research at 47 companies around the world, including Citibank, HP, Hitachi, Infosys, Intel, LG Electronics, Novartis, Philips, Samsung, Siemens, Vodafone, and Xerox. In 2004 we teamed up with Booz & Company to conduct a global survey that was completed by 186 companies from 19 countries and 17 sectors, with a combined innovation spend of more than US$78 billion. We draw on that work to present a set of guidelines for successfully managing global innovation projects.

1. Start Small

One of the chief enablers of dispersed innovation is the experience of the participating sites in working on global projects. No matter how strong technical capabilities or customer knowledge may be at a particular site, employees will struggle to make a contribution to a global project commensurate with their skills if they have had experience only in colocated development. That's because on single location projects, team members benefit from collective tacit knowledge and a shared context, both of which support rich communication and help build trust and confidence among coworkers. Projects that span multiple sites and time zones are often hobbled by differences in workplace practices, communication patterns, and cultural norms. In the absence of everyday interactions and encounters, people struggle to signal trustworthiness and demonstrate competencies. Making matters worse, many teams are used to competing for resources with teams at other sites, and this creates yet another barrier to trust and collaboration between sites.

To be effective, dispersed teams have to develop a new set of collaboration competencies and establish a collaborative mind-set. This can be done by running small, dispersed projects involving just two or three sites before a project launch. Schneider Electric and Toshiba, two global electronics manufacturers, took this approach when they formed a joint venture, STI, to develop electrical drives and inverters. Although management was enthusiastic about the

Idea in Brief

Many firms struggle to exploit the innovation potential of their global networks. That's partly because they manage global projects like traditional ones. But single-location projects draw on a reservoir of shared tacit knowledge and trust that global projects lack. To get the most from dispersed innovation, managers need a different playbook.

Enabling Conditions

Global teams need collaboration competencies. These can be developed by running projects with just two or three sites before a project launch. Firms also must foster a climate of organizational stability and keep disruptions to a minimum.

Management Structures

Senior executives must have an explicit oversight role in global projects, and one site should be designated as the lead, to avoid time-consuming negotiations.

Resourcing

Companies should invest resources up front in defining the project, and must fight the urge to allocate resources on the basis of availability rather than skills and capabilities. Some knowledge overlap among sites is desirable. Firms should limit the number of external partners, as they add complexity.

Communication

The success of a global project remains dependent upon communication channels that mimic the richness of colocation.

new partnership, engineers at the two companies were not. To build trust between sites, STI organized a series of small, noncritical joint projects under the close scrutiny of senior managers. By the end of the first project, the teams had already begun to feel comfortable collaborating with colleagues at other sites. They quickly established consensus on working practices and protocols, reinforcing trust and providing a good foundation for the more complex global initiatives to come.

2. Provide a Stable Organizational Context

During periods of major organizational change, such as restructurings or acquisitions integration, the complexity of dispersed innovation escalates. Top managers are likely to be focused elsewhere within the organization, leaving their global projects orphaned. Critical decisions are frequently left hanging, and problems often go unaddressed. In a climate of organizational uncertainty, turf battles can flare up, and project team members may become concerned about job security and lose focus.

Consider a global electronics firm we'll call Elecompt. It launched a global innovation project at a time when new acquisitions were being integrated and a major reorganization of R&D was under way. Although the project was of strategic importance, management focus was understandably elsewhere. Problems came to a head when, prompted by fear of job losses, large numbers of highly skilled engineers at one site left the company, causing significant delays.

Of course, it's not possible to undertake global innovation projects only in times of sustained stability, so managers need to anticipate the possible toxic side effects of reorganization on global innovation and shelter teams as much as possible from disruptions. They should focus on creating an atmosphere of stability and bolster employees' sense of self-worth and loyalty to the firm. This will be particularly important for firms that are expanding R&D in China, where competition for talent is so intense that loyalty to employers rarely has time to develop.

3. Assign Oversight and Support Responsibility to a Senior Manager

When the knowledge base underlying a project is fragmented and project teams are scattered over multiple locations, miscommunication, conflict, and stalemates over crucial decision making are much more likely. Project teams often struggle to handle these problems constructively over a distance, especially when disagreements become personal, and so senior managers have to take on a formal role as arbiter, risk manager, support provider, and ultimate decision maker.

Contrast this with the more familiar world of single location projects, where senior managers can give the go-ahead to an innovation project and then step back and let the team get on with it. This hands-off approach works because on-site executives can rely on informal communication and feedback mechanisms to maintain oversight. Being on the spot, they're more likely to become aware of difficulties early on and can intervene when necessary to resolve them.

Companies that are smart about global innovation create an explicit role for senior executives in their projects. For example, at Essilor, a global corrective lens manufacturer, an executive team member is assigned to head up every international project. He or she monitors project progress and is responsible for making key decisions and ensuring that the project meets the firm's strategic objectives.

Essilor undertook a project to develop photochromic lenses with partners PPG and Transitions Optical. The project involved more than 20 sites around the world. To ensure first mover advantage, the schedule was extremely aggressive. Once the project was under way, it became clear that to hit the launch date, the production ramp-up phase would have to be reduced. This could be achieved only by taking shortcuts in the production validation and evaluation processes. None of the managers of the 18 production facilities were comfortable with that kind of risk.

With loose executive oversight and unclear decision rights, the project might have stalled or derailed before the issue came to the attention of senior management. But the executive responsible for the project saw the dilemma immediately and took it to the executive committee. Because time to market was critical, the committee agreed to the shortcuts and made it clear that the risk belonged to the project, not to the production sites. The problem was resolved without any disruption to the work flow, and the product was launched on schedule.

4. Use Rigorous Project Management and Seasoned Project Leaders

In addition to a fully engaged senior manager, a global innovation project requires a strong project management team to drive the project on a day-to-day basis and strong team leaders supported by robust tools and processes. These are necessary to impose discipline, structure, and a shared sense of purpose across the locations.

Firms can approach these challenges in a number of ways. Some adopt rigorous quality programs to provide formal project management for global projects. Siemens uses Design for Six Sigma to define common analytical tools, provide coaching, and set targets and timetables for feedback meetings. Those processes are then adopted across all sites.

Alternatively, firms can build a corporate project-management capability. Essilor, the lens manufacturer, has a corporate unit that runs global projects. The unit includes staff members from all functions and geographies—many of whom spend several years as project managers of global innovation efforts before returning to their area of specialty. These positions are desirable ones: Project managers value the opportunity to work closely with the senior executives assigned to their projects. And because the roles involve extensive travel and exposure to different parts of the firm, project managers leave the unit having built strong cross-cultural skills and robust relationships and networks all over the world.

It's important to note that global innovation projects are so complex that standard tools and processes don't always work well. At the joint venture STI, a project manager realized that misunderstandings resulting from e-mail communication between teams were causing the schedule to slip. With senior management support, he successfully introduced a protocol requiring that all initial communication on a topic be voice-to-voice. At the software firm Synopsys, the global development of a new product ran in parallel to the incremental development of an existing product, a traditional approach at many firms. Concerned that this would lead to an "us versus them" culture, the project manager organized work spaces to mix up the two teams.

5. Appoint a Lead Site

Each site involved in global innovation will see the project through the prism of its own contribution and context, rather than putting the bigger picture first. That's why all sites can't carry equal weight, even if their experience and expertise are equivalent; one has to be designated the lead. That site takes responsibility for delivering the project on time and on budget.

Let's compare the approaches taken by Elecompt on its global project and by Schneider on its STI joint venture with Toshiba. Each site involved in the STI project was a global leader in its field. However, the French site, which had been heavily involved in defining the new product requirements, was given responsibility for the project: coordinating the project management team, integrating the work of the other sites, and making final decisions. Having a clear lead site ensured prompt decision making and a project successfully delivered on time and on budget.

At Elecompt, each site had equal weight in making decisions and managing the project. That meant that every decision and aspect of cooperation had to be negotiated among multiple sites, at best a slow and cumbersome process. With each site defending its own corner, stalemates were common. One engineer noted that "there was an escalation of problems without corresponding solutions." Two years into the project and with renewed senior management focus, the necessary management structures were finally put in place to enable the project to progress.

6. Invest Time Defining the Innovation

Anyone who has worked on a single location project knows that the product or service delivered isn't always what was anticipated at the outset. This is actually one of the great benefits of colocation innovation. Because everyone involved is under the same roof and in frequent communication, continuous learning and adaptation can take place, allowing the design of the product or service to improve over the course of the project.

When a project is split over time zones, cultures, and languages, there is very little latitude for iterative learning. Instead, everything must be defined up front: the product or service architecture, the functionality of individual modules, and the interdependencies and interfaces between modules. In addition, process flows, timelines, and knowledge requirements need to be thoroughly understood so that everyone working on the project has the same understanding of the goals and their individual contributions to them.

Although there is a natural temptation to dive into development as soon as possible, studies show a positive correlation between investment in defining goals and technical specifications and the successful outcome of projects. In the case of Essilor's photochromic lens, despite having less than two years to deliver the new product, the project team invested nine months in defining the modules and multiple interfaces that would be handled by specialist teams from around the world, thereby building a solid foundation for success.

During the definition process, representatives from each project team were colocated for short periods of time. In addition, the constantly globe-trotting project managers held frequent on-site meetings and spent time conferring face-to-face with team members. We believe that a global project can't be effectively defined without some degree of colocation between the different functions and sites involved. Colocation builds relationships and trust up front and supports the sharing of complex ideas and concepts.

7. Allocate Resources on the Basis of Capability, Not Availability

The question of how best to staff a project rarely arises when only one location is involved: That location has presumably been chosen because the teams there have the requisite skills and experience. The effective staffing of a global project, however, requires a great deal of attention in order to select and integrate the best possible knowledge and capabilities.

But all too often, firms see global projects as an opportunity to make the most efficient use of human resources. Teams are selected not because they are the best qualified but because they are available at the time. The consequences of this approach can be seen in the Elecompt project. One of the sites, a U.S. team, was asked to develop a critical piece of software because it had the most staff availability, even though it lacked the required experience, and it struggled as a result. Eventually, when resources became available elsewhere, this module was moved to a team that had the necessary capabilities—but by then, morale had been dented, time wasted, and costs increased.

This availability approach to staffing projects completely undermines the basic rationale for global innovation—to bring together distinctive and differentiated knowledge and capabilities from around the world to create unique innovations. If teams are selected merely because they aren't doing anything else at the time rather than for their distinct capabilities, the project will take on a lot of risk for little benefit.

8. Build Enough Knowledge Overlap for Collaboration

Although sites involved in a project should be selected on the basis of the unique capabilities and knowledge they can bring, there also has to be a small degree of knowledge overlap between sites. Without this, critical interdependencies between modules may not be apparent until the integration phase, when problems are costly to rectify. This doesn't mean replicating the other sites' knowledge, but understanding enough of what they do to anticipate potential interdependencies and interfaces in the development process.

At Siemens, virtual cross-functional teams provide knowledge overlaps to help avoid such problems. Each module is developed by a specialist team and overseen by a virtual team comprising representatives from each of the other modules. This allows potential problems to be flagged and resolved as they arise.

9. Limit the Number of Subcontractors and Partners

In most innovation projects today, part of the work is outsourced or undertaken by development partners in order to access specific competencies, reduce development time, or cut costs. The final consideration in staffing global projects is selecting these external collaborators.

Managing relationships with external parties takes time and energy. So it makes sense in global projects to limit the additional complexity and management burden by keeping the number of subcontractors or partners to a minimum. And just as it's essential to use internal sites that have experience working together, it's easier and less risky to turn to external firms that are trusted and familiar. Choosing partners or subcontractors located close to one of the internal project sites will likewise reduce the potential for cross-cultural misunderstandings and will support face-to-face communication.

An example of the problems that can be caused by involving too many distant external partners in an innovation project can be clearly seen in Boeing's 787 Dreamliner project. This ambitious effort aimed to develop a new plane with significantly reduced operating costs by using innovative composite materials. The project involved over 50 main partners across the U.S., Europe, and East Asia, each charged with developing different subsections.

Coordinating that many partners was difficult, and Boeing had little insight into what was happening at each site. Integration proved extremely complex and constant modifications were required—for example, the new materials initially made it impossible to attach the wings to the fuselage. To get the project back on track, Boeing resorted to collocating its partners for six months. Although the final product was a success, it was delivered almost three years late, during which time Boeing lost orders to the Airbus A350.

10. Don't Rely Solely on Technology for Communication

In the end, the successful execution of a global project remains dependent upon communication channels that go as far as possible to replicate the richness of colocated communication. In single locations, a shared context—cultural, organizational, functional, and technological—makes it easier to discuss complex ideas and resolve problems informally. Because communication in this environment is second nature, managers tend to underestimate the challenge of scaling communication globally.

Information and communications technologies, or ICTs, including e-mail, web meetings, social media platforms, online forums, and video conferencing certainly have a role to play, but those tools shouldn't be overrelied on, because they tend to mask differences between locations, leading to misunderstandings and tension. In addition to ICTs, the communication armory for a global innovation project should include a generous travel budget for face-to-face site visits, project team meetings, and temporary transfers for key people. Also, to encourage team members to feel an allegiance and sense of belonging to a global project rather than their local site, a web of cross-site reporting lines can be put in place. This has the added advantage of forcing communication and knowledge sharing.

Successful globally integrated firms understand the importance of an extensive communications approach. Tata Communications, for example, has a highly dispersed structure that enables it to access the best competencies and market knowledge around the world. Even its top management team is dispersed across the globe. The company has invested in a raft of ICTs to support everyday collaboration, but this is in addition to hefty travel budgets for vital, regular face-to-face communication to drive projects forward, share knowledge, and reinforce trust.

———————————

Together, the 10 steps we have outlined represent the foundation for successful global innovation projects. Adopting only one or two may result in fleeting success in some projects but will not produce a stream of positive outcomes. These best practices all need to be put in place and honed over time. It's not easy to build a global innovation capability, but for companies that don't have the skills and processes in place to manage global innovation projects, the future offers a stark choice: Continue with only colocated projects, in the hope that they will fill the innovation pipeline for a few more years until global competition intensifies and makes local innovation a niche activity. Or begin building a capability in global innovation now to take advantage of lower development costs, faster time to market, and, most important, the ability to leverage dispersed knowledge to gain competitive advantage.

Originally published in October 2012. Reprint R1210F

Lost in Translation

by Fons Trompenaars and Peter Woolliams

IT DOESN'T TAKE MUCH experience of life to realize that we vary enormously in how we perceive and respond to failure, and that a great many of those perceptions and responses are shaped by the cultures in which we grew up or now work. Of course, stories about cultural differences and stereotypes have long been a staple of dinner-table conversations and the source of much amusement. But Western multinationals are sinking a huge amount of money into India, China, and Brazil, and emerging giants in those countries are setting up operations both in developed world markets and in other emerging markets. Any business with global aspirations must take seriously cultural differences in general and around failure in particular.

Those differences are a central theme in our research. Drawing on the findings of an ongoing global survey that THT Consulting has conducted over the past 30 years (the results were first published and discussed in *Riding the Waves of Culture*), we have identified the dimensions along which people from various cultures differ regarding failure. Here we discuss in detail the five most important of those dimensions and describe how some forward-looking companies are managing to reconcile cultural differences to create a powerful platform for innovation.

1. Do We Control Our Environment or Does It Control Us?

This dimension determines whether you manage failure with prevention or with response. Cultures that view the environment as *internally* controlled—by an individual or a company—believe that good design and planning can help to avoid most failures. Cultures that view the environment as *externally* controlled accept failure as inevitable and believe that survival depends on developing the skills to respond to it quickly.

We assessed the degree to which respondents in our global survey felt they had control over their lives and found considerable variation. Almost 90% of Israeli respondents and about 80% of those from the United States, Britain, Australia, and Canada felt that they had a strong degree of control over their environment. Predictably, perhaps, only 40% of the Chinese and 50% of the Russians felt they had such control. But the stereotypes don't always hold. Some 70% of people in both South Korea and Indonesia felt they had control. Clearly, there are advantages and disadvantages to both views. People who feel that control is internal see failure as a personal threat and may become authoritarian or manipulative to increase their comfort level. They may write lengthy contracts that cover every conceivable contingency and hedge every clause. But they are less wasteful, because they tend not to repeat mistakes. Cultures that are more fatalistic are also more adaptable. They respond quickly and efficiently to failure. But they tend to leave the causes of failure untreated, so they have to pick up the same pieces again and again, which can be very expensive.

Obviously, a company that combined prevention with adaptability would be a formidable competitor. Emirates, the national airline of Dubai, is a good example. During training exercises, Western pilots try to avoid failure, even though "crashing" in a simulator costs nothing. They propose changes in cockpit design and procedures and change routes to minimize the likelihood of disaster. By contrast, Arab pilots who are given a chance to "fail" without consequences will take risks and respond to them. They want to experience a crisis situation—such as how the controls feel seconds before going into a stall. They'll pass through a virtual cloud rather than around or over it. Emirates learns from pilots of both kinds to prevent failures and improve responses to them, making it one of the safest airlines in the world.

Idea in Brief

People vary enormously in how they perceive and respond to failure, and those perceptions and responses are shaped by the cultures in which they grew up or now work. Western multinationals are sinking a huge amount of money into India, China, and Brazil, and emerging giants in those countries are setting up operations in world markets as well. Any business with global aspirations must take seriously cultural differences in general and around failure in particular. Drawing on the findings of a global survey that has been ongoing for 30 years, Trompenaars and Woolliams have identified the dimensions along which people from various cultures differ regarding failure. They discuss the five most important of those dimensions: (1) Do we view our environment as internally or externally controlled? (2) Which is more important—rules or relationships? (3) Are failures the responsibility of the individual or of the team? (4) How much do we identify with our failures? (5) Do we grant status according to performance or to position? The authors describe how some forward-looking companies are managing to reconcile cultural differences to create a powerful platform for innovation.

2. What's More Important, Rules or Relationships?

How strictly we adhere to rules and how eagerly we make them vary greatly from culture to culture. *Rule-centered* societies like the United States and Britain feel that general rules should have global application and that all comers should compete on a level playing field. *Relationship-centered* countries like China, Russia, and India value bonds with family and friends above abstract rules: Particular circumstances and the people involved may dictate the response to a situation.

Countries in the former category probably better satisfy the desire for distributive justice, but they may become obsessed with rules and regulations—which explains in part why the United States has so many more lawyers than Japan does. Countries in the latter category tend to resolve failure privately, through relationships. The Swiss, North Americans, and Australians are the most rule-oriented, with 70% to 80% of respondents believing that exceptions to rules should not be made to help friends. In the BRIC countries, by contrast, only 25% to 40% would put the rule above the person.

We often see these approaches collide in global organizations, usually in interactions between a headquarters focused on rules and principles and local offices that are highly sensitive to their relationship networks. Typically the local offices appear to conform to rules and principles while actually following local customs. As long as broad financial expectations are met, no one asks questions. But that means the organization as a whole cannot learn from local successes and failures.

A relationship-centered organization, with its tolerance of failure, can encourage innovation and learning. But it may also be wasteful, and its employees may be reluctant to compete with friends, curtailing entrepreneurial opportunities. A rules-centered organization provides clarity and, often, greater cost efficiency. But it also breeds inflexibility and mountains of red tape.

Companies can combine the virtues of both by recognizing that rules and exceptions are mutually sustaining. An exception to a rule may contain the seed of a new rule or illuminate the limits of the old one. Using a technique called "management by exception," which draws attention to any surprise event falling outside existing rules and expectations, managers can strengthen some rules and obviate others. And the existence of rules helps to make exceptional relationships meaningful.

A case in point was provided by a global financial services firm we advised. The company, which was based in Germany, stated that its main value was integrity. But its employees' interpretation of "integrity" varied enormously. Americans saw it as sticking to principles even if that meant being hard on friends. Koreans and many other relationship-centered employees believed that it was best expressed by helping friends even if that meant bending a principle or two.

In the course of several workshops, we uncovered ways of reconciling these two views. It was a Brazilian employee of the firm who pointed out that bending a rule for a friend can be used to motivate that friend. Suppose your friend has been performing badly.

You can say you will fudge his assessment, but only this one time. Indeed, the performance criteria at his next review will actually be tougher—though you are prepared to mentor him if he's willing to try to improve and meet them. In this way you demonstrate both loyalty to your friend and commitment to the rules. Meanwhile, he is motivated to perform better—which is essentially what you hoped to achieve in the first place.

3. Are Failures the Responsibility of the Individual or the Team?

In *individualistic* societies like the United States, workers are very independent and even compete with their colleagues. Although internal competition can be organizationally toxic, it can also be highly productive, especially in businesses that compete on their ability to sell. Naming a Best Salesperson of the Quarter at company award ceremonies helps to boost sales targets.

At the other end of the spectrum are *communitarian* countries, in which people take responsibility for errors as a group, even when only one member is involved. At the Indonesian subsidiary of a U.S. multinational we studied, a local worker had made a serious error that forced the company to redo an entire production batch. The expatriate unit manager asked the Indonesian plant director who had made the error and what action was being taken against her. The manager was amazed when the plant director claimed not to know, saying, "The whole work group has accepted responsibility."

"But if everyone is responsible, then in effect no one is," the manager argued. "They are simply protecting one another's bad work."

"That is not how we see it," the plant manager replied. "The woman concerned was so upset that she went home. She tried to resign. Two of her coworkers had to coax her back again. The group knows she was responsible, and she feels shame. The group also knows that she was new and they did not help her enough or look out for her or see that she was properly trained. That is why the whole group has apologized. They are willing to apologize to you publicly."

A Failure Culture Survey

ASKING EMPLOYEES THE FOLLOWING simple questions can help you assess how failure is viewed across your organization.

1. Are failures a fact of life or can they be avoided by planning?

2. What would you do if a friend made a professional mistake on which you needed to report publicly?

3. Is it individual creativity or team consensus that is most important for avoiding mistakes?

4. Do you address criticism to the task or to the person?

5. Is the seriousness of a mistake affected by the person who made it or not?

6. Are failures attributed to the person or team involved or to the department head?

As the story illustrates, communitarianism can provide a nurturing learning environment. Through team membership we support people to become better individual workers. At the same time, someone who "lets the group down" will experience shame in a communitarian culture. The downside, of course, is that companies dominated by a sense of the group can choke off individual creativity and the striving for personal excellence.

For communitarianism to work well, a group's interests and values must strongly align with the company's objectives—as they clearly did in the Indonesian example. But it is also important that a group's learning spreads, which may mean assigning responsibility for a failure to an individual. In such a case it may be possible to remove the stigma by redefining the failure as a learning opportunity.

What we call "co-opetition" can bring some communitarianism to an individualistic company. At IBM, for example, in addition to receiving bonuses based on their volume, salespeople are rewarded for making good presentations to colleagues on lessons learned from client interactions. The group's performance has risen by 30% since this program was introduced.

We asked our survey respondents whether mistakes like the one made by the Indonesian worker should be borne by the individual or by the group. Russians turned out to be the most individualistic: Almost 70% would blame the individual. Australians (58%) and Americans (54%) came in second and third. Danes were significantly more individualistic (53%) than either the British (48%) or the Dutch (43%). Among the most group-oriented countries, China was slightly more individualistic (36%) than India (35%), Japan, and Brazil (both below 35%), which was unexpected.

4. How Much Do We Identify with Our Failures?

People in *non-identifying* cultures are not afraid of failure. They compartmentalize, viewing a failure as simply an idea that didn't work. Furthermore, they celebrate failure as a learning opportunity. They are, however, more likely to jump to conclusions too quickly, and may waste a lot of energy. For people in *identifying* cultures, failure is a bigger deal. When we asked our survey respondents whether they blamed the person or the idea, we found that 72% of the Dutch and 66% of the Americans blamed the idea, whereas only 31% of the Indians, 29% of the Germans, 24% of the Chinese, and 12% of the Japanese did.

Consider the dynamic we observed between American and German engineers at the semiconductor giant AMD, which we advised shortly after it had set up operations in Germany. The U.S. semiconductor industry can attribute much of its success to the integration of individual creativity with teamwork and to the successful use of failures. When AMD arrived in Dresden, programs were executed in a stereotypical American manner: Videos, workshops, and pep talks were done the "Silicon way" and combined with brainstorming sessions in the so-called war room.

When we interviewed American employees, we heard many complaints about the slowness, lack of creativity, and risk-averseness of their German counterparts when it came to exploratory ideas. The Germans, in turn, claimed that the Americans were too hasty in their behavior, throwing clearly underdeveloped ideas into brainstorming sessions. The reason for this tension quickly emerged in our workshops. Because the Americans separated the ideas from the people, they readily accepted criticism during a brainstorming session: "My idea was hacked into pieces. No problem. On with the next idea." But to the Germans, this approach was misguided: "All that exaggerated business about the importance of effective meetings and brainstorming. Let's just do our homework and everything will work out."

AMD found a way to reconcile these views. In hindsight the solution seems simple. Time-outs were built into each meeting, which allowed the Germans to swap and criticize ideas in private and in German. Failures in the smaller, familiar group were acceptable. Their ideas were then collated on Post-it notes and shared with the Americans. The Americans were astonished at the resultant German creativity.

5. Do We Grant Status According to Performance or Position?

In *achieving* cultures, people value others according to their performance, whereas *ascribing* cultures emphasize a person's position in the organization and the society. This difference plays a role in determining the extent to which people are willing to show initiative and risk failure.

In achieving cultures, people take a lot of personal initiative—but they are often very protective of their achievements, which can play out in the broader culture as a strong sense of property rights and much litigiousness. And if achievement is valued too highly, people may exaggerate their own successes, take credit for those of others, or even game the system. (One of us was at a leading business school recently and came upon an MBA student leaving the library with eight books. When asked why he had so many, the student explained that he was more interested in making sure no one else read them than in reading them himself.) In an overachieving culture, innovation may be stifled when the willingness to risk failure is moderated by a fear of not achieving. To prevent abuse, managers have to be very careful and visibly impartial in assigning credit for successes and failures.

In ascribing cultures, people avoid taking responsibility for actions when their superiors are around, because they gain little—and may actually incite hostility—for successes, whereas they are vulnerable if they make mistakes. Employees first discuss their actions with the boss; once they get the go-ahead, the boss takes responsibility for success or failure. In an achieving culture, if the goal demands it, people will take action and inform the boss later. If things go wrong, the boss will judge whether the risk was reasonably assessed and the action had the potential to achieve the goal.

We heard the following story from the head of process control at a British dairy company. A man we'll call Malcolm, one of the plant's best process operators, knew—like his colleagues— how to read the meters and intervene when necessary. What made him special was his well-developed intuition. If he stopped the production process straightaway when he sensed something was odd, his prompt action saved the company money in 99 out of 100 cases. On night shifts, when his boss wasn't around, he would take the initiative, but on day shifts he would go to his boss for direction. Telling him that he was causing a lot of unnecessary loss by delaying a shutdown for even five minutes didn't change his behavior. The company was able to overcome Malcolm's hesitation by giving him the title of supervisor, empowering him to decide when to shut production down whether his boss was there or not.

A similar gambit worked for an achievement-oriented U.S. bank operating in highly ascribing Argentina. When the American manager of the Argentinean subsidiary complained about the low motivation of his administrative staffers, we advised him to take a look at their job titles, which had been imported from the United States: Departmental Secretary I, II, and III. After the highest-ranking secretary was promoted to Personal Assistant and the others were given titles that made clear the positions of those for whom they worked, a more positive atmosphere quickly developed. The manager told us, "Not only was it in line with their culture, but best of all, it did not affect my budget."

———

Of course, countries—and even industries—are not the only units of cultural comparison, and they may conceal a wide variation across some of the dimensions. The failure culture of a Japanese car company, for example, may resemble GM's more than Sony's. Variations within companies may arise from people's functional affiliations or hierarchical status. To manage failure as part of a learning strategy, therefore, you must understand just where the variations are most salient in your company. You'll need to conduct research at many levels across your business units, distinguishing by function, business line, hierarchical status, and geography. But at any organizational level, the cultural dimensions we have described here will give you a strong framework for your enquiry.

Originally published in April 2011. Reprint W1104A

The Right Way to Manage Expats

by J. Stewart Black and Hal B. Gregersen

IN TODAY'S GLOBAL ECONOMY, having a workforce that is fluent in the ways of the world isn't a luxury. It's a competitive necessity. No wonder nearly 80% of midsize and large companies currently send professionals abroad—and 45% plan to increase the number they have on assignment.

But international assignments don't come cheap. On average, expatriates cost two to three times what they would in an equivalent position back home. A fully loaded expatriate package including benefits and cost-of-living adjustments costs anywhere from $300,000 to $1 million annually, probably the single largest expenditure most companies make on any one individual except for the CEO.

The fact is, however, that most companies get anemic returns on their expat investments. Over the past decade, we have studied the management of expatriates at about 750 U.S., European, and Japanese companies. We asked both the expatriates themselves and the executives who sent them abroad to evaluate their experiences. In addition, we looked at what happened after expatriates returned home. Was their tenure worthwhile from a personal and organizational standpoint?

Overall, the results of our research were alarming. We found that between 10% and 20% of all U.S. managers sent abroad returned early because of job dissatisfaction or difficulties in adjusting to a foreign country. Of those who stayed for the duration, nearly one-third did not perform up to the expectations of their superiors. And perhaps most problematic, one-fourth of those who completed an assignment left their company, often to join a competitor, within one year after repatriation. That's a turnover rate double that of managers who did not go abroad.

If getting the most out of your expats is so important, why do so many companies get it so wrong? The main reason seems to be that many executives assume that the rules of good business are the same everywhere. In other words, they don't believe they need to—or should have to—engage in special efforts for their expats.

Take the expat assignment process. Executives know that negotiation tactics and marketing strategies can vary from culture to culture. Most do not believe, however, that the variance is sufficient to warrant the expense of programs designed to select or train candidates for international assignments.

Further, once expats are in place, executives back home usually are not inclined to coddle their well-paid representatives. When people are issued first-class tickets on a luxury liner, they're not supposed to complain about being at sea.

Finally, people at the home office find it difficult to imagine that returning expats need help readjusting after just a few years away. They don't see why people who've been given an extended period to explore the Left Bank or the Forbidden City should get a hero's welcome. As a result of such thinking, the only time companies pay special attention to their expats is when something goes spectacularly wrong. And by then, it's too little, too late.

Of course, some companies do engage in serious efforts to make foreign assignments beneficial both for the employees and the organization. Very often, however, such companies consign the responsibility of expat selection, training, and support to the human resources department. Few HR managers—only 11%, according to our research—have ever worked abroad themselves; most have little understanding of a global assignment's unique personal and professional challenges. As a result, they often get bogged down in

Idea in Brief

In the global economy, having a workforce that is fluent in the ways of the world is a competitive necessity. That's why more and more companies are sending more and more professionals abroad. But international assignments don't come cheap: On average, expatriates cost a company two to three times what they would cost in equivalent positions back home. Most companies, however, get anemic returns on their expat investments. The authors discovered that an alarming number of assignments fail in one way or another—some expats return home early, others finish but don't perform as well as expected, and many leave their companies within a year of repatriation. To find out why, the authors recently focused on the small number of companies that manage their expats successfully. They found that all those companies follow three general practices: (1) When they send people abroad, the goal is not just to put out fires. Once expats have doused the flames, they are expected to generate new knowledge for the organization or to acquire skills that will help them become leaders. (2) They assign overseas posts to people whose technical skills are matched or exceeded by their cross-cultural skills. (3) They recognize that repatriation is a time of upheaval for most expats, and they use a variety of programs to help their people readjust. Companies that follow these practices share a conviction that sustained growth rests on the shoulders of individuals with international experience. As a result, they are poised to capture tomorrow's global market opportunities by making their investments in international assignments successful today.

the administrative minutiae of international assignments instead of capturing strategic opportunities.

Over the past several years, we have concentrated on examining the small number of companies that have compiled a winning track record in the process of managing their expats. Their people overseas report a high degree of job satisfaction and back that up with strong performance. These companies also hold on to their expats long after they return home. GE Medical Systems, for example, has all but eliminated unwanted turnover after repatriation and has seen its international sales expand from 10% to more than 50% of its total sales during the last ten years.

The companies that manage their expats effectively come in many sizes and from a wide range of industries. Yet we have found that they all follow three general practices:

When making international assignments, they focus on knowledge creation and global leadership development. Many companies send people abroad to reward them, to get them out of the way, or to fill an immediate business need. At companies that manage the international assignment process well, however, people are given foreign posts for two related reasons: to generate and transfer knowledge, to develop their global leadership skills, or to do both.

They assign overseas posts to people whose technical skills are matched or exceeded by their cross-cultural abilities. Companies that manage expats wisely do not assume that people who have succeeded at home will repeat that success abroad. They assign international posts to individuals who not only have the necessary technical skills but also have indicated that they would be likely to live comfortably in different cultures.

They end expatriate assignments with a deliberate repatriation process. Most executives who oversee expat employees view their return home as a nonissue. The truth is, repatriation is a time of major upheaval, professionally and personally, for two-thirds of expats. Companies that recognize this fact help their returning people by providing them with career guidance and enabling them to put their international experience to work.

Let's explore the practices in turn, illustrating them with companies that have put them to good use over the past several years.

Sending People for the Right Reasons

For as long as companies have been sending people abroad, many have been doing so for the wrong reasons—that is, for reasons that make little long-term business sense. Foreign assignments in glamorous locales such as Paris and London have been used to reward favored employees; posts to distant lands have been used as dumping grounds for the mediocre. But in most cases, companies send people abroad to fill a burning business need: to fight a competitor gaining market share in Brazil, to open a factory in China, to keep the computers running in Portugal.

Immediate business demands cannot be ignored. But the companies that manage their expats effectively view foreign assignments with an eye on the long term. Even when people are sent abroad to extinguish fires, they are expected to plant forests when the embers are cool. They are expected to go beyond pressing problems either to generate new knowledge for the organization or to acquire skills that will help them become leaders.

Imagine a large Canadian company that wants to open a telephone-making plant in Vietnam. It would certainly send a manager who knows how to manufacture phones and how to get a greenfield facility up and running quickly. The manager's performance rating and compensation would reflect those objectives, but that's where most companies would stop. Companies that manage their expats effectively, however, would require more of the manager in Vietnam. Once the plant was established, he would be expected to transfer his knowledge to local professionals—and to learn from them, too. Together, they would be expected to generate innovative ideas.

Nokia, the world's second largest manufacturer of mobile phones, is a good example of a company that effectively uses international assignments to generate knowledge. Unlike most large technology companies, Nokia does not rely on a central R&D function. Instead, it operates 36 centers in 11 countries—from Finland to China to the United States. Senior executives scan their global workforce for engineers and designers who are likely to generate new ideas when combined into a team. They bring these people together in an R&D center for assignments of up to two years, with the explicit objective of inventing new products. The approach works well: Nokia continues to grab global market share by rapidly turning new ideas into successful commercial products, such as the Nokia 6100 series mobile telephones that were launched last year in Beijing and have quickly captured a leading position in markets around the world.

Other companies have more need to focus on the second reason for international assignments: to develop global leadership skills. Such companies would concur with a recent observation by GE's CEO: "The Jack Welch of the future cannot be like me. I've spent my entire career in the United States. The next head of GE will be somebody who has spent time in Bombay, in Hong Kong, in Buenos Aires." An executive cannot develop a global perspective on business or become comfortable with foreign cultures by staying at headquarters or taking short business trips abroad. Such intangibles come instead as a result of having spent more than one sustained period working abroad.

Indeed, the only way to change fundamentally how people think about doing business globally is by having them work abroad for several months at a time. Everyone has a mental map of the world—a set of ingrained assumptions about what people are like and how the world works. But our maps may not be able to point us in the right direction when we try to use them in uncharted territory. Consider the case of a tall American businessman who, during a recent trip to Japan, dined at a traditional restaurant. Upon entering, he bumped his head on the doorjamb. The next day, the same thing happened. It was only on the third time that he remembered to duck. People on international assignments hit their heads on doorjambs many times over the years. Eventually, they learn to duck—to expect that the world abroad will be different from the one they had imagined. Hard experience has rearranged their mental maps or, at the very least, expanded the boundaries on their maps.

It is with such a broadened view of the world that global leaders are made. A vice president for Disney, for example, was posted in 1993 to EuroDisney, the company's struggling theme park just outside Paris. Stephen Burke arrived in France with the same mental map of the company as the senior managers at home. He believed, for instance, that families and alcohol do not mix at Disney theme parks. But after living in France for several months, Burke came to see what an affront EuroDisney's no-alcohol policy was to most of its potential local customers. A glass of wine with lunch was as French as a cheeseburger was American. Further, Burke came to see that Disney's lack of focus on tour operators—a more important distribution channel in Europe than in North America—made it inconvenient to book reservations for complete vacation packages, which many Europeans prefer to arrange.

With his new perspective on the local market, Burke pushed hard to persuade Disney's top management to sell wine at its French park and to create complete vacation packages for tour operators. He succeeded. Because of those and other changes, attendance and hotel occupancy soon skyrocketed, and EuroDisney posted its first operational profit. Burke told us afterward, "The assignment to EuroDisney caused me to challenge long-held assumptions that were based on my experiences and career at Disney. After living in France, I came to look at the world quite differently."

The two principal goals of international assignments—generation of knowledge and development of global leaders—are not mutually exclusive. But it is unlikely that an international posting will allow a company to achieve both goals in every case or to an equal degree. Not every employee going abroad has abundant knowledge to share or the right stuff to be the company's future CEO. What matters, however, is that executives explicitly know beforehand why they are sending a person overseas—and that the reason goes beyond an immediate business problem.

Just as important, it is critical that expats themselves know the rationale for their assignments. Are they being sent abroad to generate knowledge or to develop their leadership skills? At the effective companies we studied, this kind of information helps expats focus on the right objectives in the right measure. For example, a communications company recently transferred one of its top lean-manufacturing experts from Asia to the United States. His task was to help managers understand and implement the practices that had been perfected in Singapore and Japan. The company's senior executives did not expect him to hone his leadership capabilities because they did not believe that he would ascend the corporate ranks. Knowing the main purpose of his posting, the expert was able to focus his energy on downloading his knowledge to other managers. Moreover, he did not build up unrealistic expectations that he would be promoted after returning home.

Companies with foreign operations will always face unexpected crises from time to time. But the companies that reap the most from sending their people abroad recognize that international assignments can't just be about sending in the medics. They must also be about ensuring the organization's health over the long term.

Sending the Right People

Just as managers often send people abroad for the wrong reasons, they frequently send the wrong people. Not because they send people who don't have the necessary technical skills. Indeed, technical skill is frequently the main reason that people are selected for open posts. But managers often send people who lack the ability to adjust to different customs, perspectives, and business practices. In other words, they send people who are capable but culturally illiterate.

Companies that have a strong track record with expats put a candidate's openness to new cultures on an equal footing with the person's technical know-how. After all, successfully navigating within your own business environment and culture does not guarantee that you can maneuver successfully in another one. We know, for instance, of a senior manager at a U.S. carmaker who was an expert at negotiating contracts with his company's steel suppliers. When transferred to Korea to conduct similar deals, the man's confrontational style did nothing but offend the consensus-minded Koreans—to the point where suppliers would not even speak to him directly. What was worse, the man was unwilling to change his way of doing business. He was soon called back to the company's home office, and his replacement spent a year undoing the damage he left in his wake.

How do you weed out people like the man who failed in Korea? The companies that manage expats successfully use a variety of tools to assess cultural sensitivity, from casual observation to formal testing. Interestingly, however, almost all evaluate people early in their careers in order to eliminate some from the potential pool of expats and help others build cross-cultural skills.

Although the companies differ in how they conduct their assessments, our research shows that they seek the following similar characteristics in their expats:

A drive to communicate

Most expats will try to communicate with local people in their new country, but people who end up being successful in their jobs are those that don't give up after early attempts either fail or embarrass them. To identify such people, the most effective companies in our research scanned their ranks for employees who were both enthusiastic and extroverted in conversation, and not afraid to try out their fractured French or talk with someone whose English was weak.

Broad-based sociability

The tendency for many people posted overseas is to stick with a small circle of fellow expats. By contrast, successful global managers establish social ties to the local residents, from shopkeepers to government officials. There is no better source for insights into a local market and no better way to adjust to strange surroundings.

Cultural flexibility

It is human nature to gravitate toward the familiar—that's why many Americans overseas find themselves eating lunch at McDonald's. But the expats who add the most value to their companies—by staying for the duration and being open to local market trends—are those who willingly experiment with different customs. In India, such people eat dal and chapatis for lunch; in Brazil, they follow the fortunes of the local jai alai team.

Cosmopolitan orientation

Expats with a cosmopolitan mind-set intuitively understand that different cultural norms have value and meaning to those who practice them. Companies that send the right people abroad have identified individuals who respect diverse viewpoints; they live and let live.

A collaborative negotiation style

When expats negotiate with foreigners, the potential for conflict is much higher than it is when they are dealing with compatriots. Different cultures can hold radically different expectations about the way negotiations should be conducted. Thus a collaborative negotiation style, which can be important enough in business at home, becomes absolutely critical abroad.

Consider the approach taken by the vice chairman of Huntsman Corporation, a private chemicals company based in Salt Lake City with sales of $4.75 billion. Over the last five years, Jon Huntsman, Jr., has developed an informal but highly successful method for assessing cultural aptitudes in his employees. He regularly asks managers that he thinks have global leadership potential to accompany him on international trips, even if immediate business needs don't justify the expense. During such trips, he takes the managers to local restaurants, shopping areas, and side streets and observes their behavior. Do they approach the strange and unusual sights, sounds, smells, and tastes with curiosity or do they look for the nearest Pizza Hut? Do they try to communicate with local shopkeepers or do they hustle back to the Hilton?

Huntsman also observes how managers act among foreigners at home. In social settings, he watches to see if they seek out the foreign guests or talk only with people they already know. During negotiations with foreigners, he gauges his managers' ability to take a collaborative rather than a combative approach.

Although time consuming and sometimes costly, Huntsman's approach to screening potential expats is actually remarkably efficient. He is able to assess candidates before the pressures of an impending international problem make a quick decision necessary. Consequently, he makes fewer expensive mistakes when choosing whom to send abroad.

Other companies, such as LG Group, a $70 billion Korean conglomerate, take a more formal approach to assessing candidates for foreign assignments. Early in their careers, candidates complete a survey of about 100 questions designed to rate their preparation for global assignments and their cross-cultural skills. Afterward,

LG employees and their managers discuss how specific training courses or future on-the-job experiences could help them enhance their strengths and overcome their weaknesses. From this discussion, a personalized development plan and timetable are generated. Because LG's potential expats are given time to develop their skills, about 97% of them succeed in meeting the company's expectations when they are eventually sent on international assignments.

The surveys used by LG were purchased from an outside company and cost from $300 to $500 per person. Other organizations develop them in-house, with the help of their training or HR departments. In either case, the survey questions generally ask people not to evaluate their own characteristics but to describe their past behavior. For example, they might be asked when they had last eaten a meal from a cuisine that was unfamiliar to them.

A third approach to identifying potential expats is used by Colgate-Palmolive, which has about 70% of its sales outside the United States and decades of international experience. To fill its entry-level marketing positions, the company recruits students from universities or business schools who can demonstrate an ability to handle cross-cultural situations. They may have already worked or lived abroad and will at the very least have traveled extensively; they will often be able to speak a foreign language. In this way, Colgate-Palmolive leverages the investment that other companies have made in an employee's first experience abroad.

Colgate-Palmolive takes a similarly cautious approach once such promising young people are on staff. Instead of sending them on long assignments abroad, it sends them on a series of training stints lasting 6 to 18 months. These assignments do not come with the costly benefits that are provided to high-level expats, such as allowances for housing and a car. This strategy means the company can provide young managers with a broad range of overseas experience. One manager hired in the United States, for example, spent time in the Czech Republic and the Baltic states and recently became country manager in Ukraine—all before celebrating his thirtieth birthday.

Companies face a trade-off between the accuracy and the cost of expat assessment. Although Colgate-Palmolive's approach is probably the most accurate way to assess an individual's potential to succeed on international assignments, it comes with a substantial price tag. That approach is probably most appropriate for a multinational that needs a large cadre of global managers. For companies with lesser workforce requirements, the less costly approaches of Huntsman and LG may make more sense. In any case, the key to success is having a systematic way of assessing the cross-cultural aptitudes of people you may want to send abroad.

Finishing the Right Way

Virtually every effective company we studied took the matter of repatriation seriously. Most companies, however, do not. Consider the findings of our research: about one-third of the expats we surveyed were still filling temporary assignments three months after coming home. More than three-quarters felt that their permanent position upon returning home was a demotion from their posting abroad, and 61% said that they lacked opportunities to put their foreign experience to work. No wonder the average turnover rate of returning professionals reaches 25%. We know of one company that over a two-year period lost all the managers it sent on international assignments within a year of their return—25 people in all. It might just as well have written a check for $50 million and tossed it to the winds.

The story of a senior engineer from a European electronics company is typical. The man was sent to Saudi Arabia on a four-year assignment, at a cost to his employers of about $4 million. During those four years, he learned fluent Arabic, gained new technical skills, and made friends with important businesspeople in the Saudi community. But upon returning home, the man was shocked to find himself frequently scolded that "the way things were done in Saudi Arabia has nothing to do with the way we do things at headquarters." Worse, he was kept waiting almost nine months for a permanent assignment which, when it came, gave him less authority than he had had abroad. Not surprisingly, the engineer left to join a direct competitor a few months later and ended up using the knowledge and skills he had acquired in Saudi Arabia against his former employer.

International assignments end badly for several reasons. First, although employers give little thought to their return, expats believe that a successful overseas assignment is an achievement that deserves recognition. They want to put their new skills and knowledge to use and are often disappointed both by the blasé attitude at headquarters toward their return and by their new jobs. That disappointment can be particularly strong for senior expats who have gotten used to the independence of running a foreign operation. As one U.K. expatriate recently observed, "If you have been the orchestra conductor overseas, it is very difficult to accept a position as second fiddle back home."

Changes in and out of the office can also make homecoming difficult. The company may have reshuffled its top management, reorganized its reporting structure, or even reshaped its culture. Old mentors may have moved on, leaving the returning employee to deal with new decision makers and power brokers. Things change in people's personal lives, too. Friends may have moved away, figuratively or literally. Children may find it hard to settle back into school or relate to old playmates.

The effective companies in our research used straightforward processes to solve these problems. At Monsanto, for example, the head office starts thinking about the next assignments for returning expats three to six months before they will return. As a first step, an HR officer and a line manager who is senior to the expat—both with international experience—assess the skills that the expat has gained during her experience overseas. They also review potential job openings within Monsanto. At the same time, the expat herself writes a report that includes a self-assessment and describes career goals. The three then meet and decide which of the available jobs best fits the expat's capabilities and the organization's needs.

In the six years since it introduced the system, Monsanto has dramatically reduced the turnover rate of its returning expatriates. And because returning employees participate in the process, they feel valued and treated fairly—even if they don't get their job of first choice.

Along with finding their returning expats suitable jobs, effective companies also prepare them for changes in their personal and professional landscapes. For example, the oil and gas company Unocal offers all expats and their families a daylong debriefing program upon their return. The program focuses on common repatriation difficulties, from communicating with colleagues who have not worked abroad to helping children fit in again with their peers. The participants watch videos of past expats and their families discussing their experiences. That sets the stage for a live discussion. In many cases, participants end up sharing tips for coping with repatriation, such as keeping a journal. The journal is useful, many returning expats say, because it helps them examine the sources of their frustrations and anxieties, which in turn helps them think about what they might do to deal with them better.

Although participants find repatriation programs useful, it is seldom cost effective for a company to provide them in-house unless its volume of international assignments is heavy. Most companies that offer such programs outsource them to professional training companies or form consortiums with other companies to share the costs. Effective companies have realized that the money they spend on these programs is a small price to pay for retaining people with global insight and experience.

Companies that manage their expats successfully follow the three practices that make the assignments work from beginning to end. They focus on creating knowledge and developing global leadership skills; they make sure that candidates have cross-cultural skills to match their technical abilities; and they prepare people to make the transition back to their home offices.

Given the poor record that most companies have when it comes to managing expats, it's probably no surprise that we often encounter organizations in which none of the three practices are at work. Some companies, however, are committed to one or two of the practices, and so the question arises, Do you have to follow all three to see a payback on your expat investment? The answer, our research would suggest, is yes. The practices not only reinforce one another, they also cover the entire expat experience, from assignment to return home.

Consider the dividends reaped by Honda of America Manufacturing, perhaps one of the best examples of a company that implements all three practices. Honda starts expat assignments with clear strategic objectives such as the development of a new car model or improved supplier relations. Assignees then complete a survey to identify personal strengths and weaknesses related to the upcoming assignment. Six months before an expat is scheduled to return home, the company initiates an active matchmaking process to locate a suitable job for that person; a debriefing interview is conducted upon repatriation to capture lessons learned from the assignment.

As a result of Honda's integrated approach, nearly all of its expats consistently perform at or above expectations, and the turnover rate for returning employees is less than 5%. Most important, its expats consistently attain the key strategic objectives established at the beginning of each assignment.

Companies like Honda, GE, and Nokia have learned how to reap the full value of international assignments. Their CEOs share a conviction that sustained global growth rests on the shoulders of key individuals, particularly those with international experience. As a result, those companies are poised to capture tomorrow's global market opportunities by making their international assignments—the largest single investments in executive development that they will make—financially successful today.

Originally published in March–April 1999. Reprint 99201

About the Contributors

KRISTIN BEHFAR is an assistant professor at the Paul Merage School of Business at the University of California, Irvine.

J. STEWART BLACK is managing director at the Center for Global Assignments, a research institute and consulting firm in San Diego, California. He is the coauthor, with Hal B. Gregersen, of *So You're Going Overseas* and *So You're Coming Home*, handbooks for expatriates (Global Business Publishers, 1998 and 1999).

JEANNE BRETT is the DeWitt W. Buchanan, Jr., Distinguished Professor of Dispute Resolution and Organizations and the director of the Dispute Resolution Research Center at Northwestern University's Kellogg School of Management in Evanston, Illinois.

THOMAS DONALDSON is a professor at the Wharton School of the University of Pennsylvania in Philadelphia, where he teaches business ethics. He wrote *The Ethics of International Business* (Oxford University Press, 1989) and is the coauthor, with Thomas W. Dunfee, of *The Ties That Bind* (Harvard Business School Press, 1997).

YVES L. DOZ is the Solvay Chaired Professor of Technological Innovation at INSEAD. He is the coauthor (with Keeley Wilson) of *Managing Global Innovation* (Harvard Business Review Press, 2012).

P. CHRISTOPHER EARLEY is a professor and the chair of the Department of Organizational Behavior at the London Business School.

ROBIN J. ELY is an associate professor at Columbia University's School of International and Public Affairs in New York City. Her research and teaching focuses on the influence of race, gender, and ethnicity on career dynamics and organizational effectiveness.

HAL B. GREGERSEN is an associate professor of international management at Brigham Young University's Marriott School of Management in Provo, Utah. He is the coauthor, with J. Stewart Black, of *So*

You're Going Overseas and *So You're Coming Home*, handbooks for expatriates (Global Business Publishers, 1998 and 1999).

HAE-JUNG HONG is an assistant professor at Rouen Business School in France.

MARY C. KERN is an assistant professor at the Zicklin School of Business at Baruch College in New York.

ERIN MEYER is an affiliate professor in organizational behavior, specializing in cross-cultural management, at INSEAD in Fontainebleau, France. She is the author of *The Culture Map: Breaking Through the Invisible Boundaries of Global Business* (PublicAffairs, 2014).

ELAINE MOSAKOWSKI is a professor of management at the University of Colorado at Boulder.

TSEDAL NEELEY is an assistant professor in the organizational behavior unit at Harvard Business School.

DAVID A. THOMAS is an associate professor at the Harvard Business School in Boston, Massachusetts. His research and teaching focus on the influence of race, gender, and ethnicity on career dynamics and organizational effectiveness.

FONS TROMPENAARS is a cofounder of Trompenaars Hampden-Turner Consulting, based in Amsterdam and London, and a coauthor, with Charles Hampden-Turner, of *Riding the Waves of Culture* (McGraw-Hill, 1993).

KEELEY WILSON is a senior research fellow at INSEAD in Fontainebleau, France. She is the coauthor (with Yves L. Doz) of *Managing Global Innovation* (Harvard Business Review Press, 2012).

PETER WOOLLIAMS is a partner with Trompenaars Hampden-Turner Consulting, based in Amsterdam and London, and an emeritus professor at Anglia Ruskin University in the UK.

Index

absolutism, 88-89
accents, 20, 22-23. *See also* language
  fluency
access-and-legitimacy paradigm,
  49-50, 57-60, 62. *See also*
  diversity
adaptation
  to cultural differences, 83-84
  in global business, 35-36, 37
  for multicultural teams, 20, 25,
  26-28
affirmative action, 52. *See also*
  diversity
AMD, 135-136
assimilation, 49, 50, 52-57, 62
authority, attitudes toward, 24,
  78, 80-81

basic rights. *See* core values
bribery, 90, 98, 99
bureaucracy, 65
business practices, in foreign
  settings, 85-102

codes of conduct, 93-95, 100, 102
Colgate-Palmolive, 149-150
collaboration, 118-119, 125, 148
colocation, 117, 123-124
communication
  direct versus indirect, 18-19, 20,
  22
  in English language, 103-116
  language barriers, 22-23, 41-42,
  106
  in low-context versus
  high-context cultures, 76
  technology, 126-127

communitarian countries,
  133-135
company culture, 1, 64, 68-69, 92,
  93-95
company structure, 65
competitive advantage, 35-36, 37,
  58, 106
confidence, cultural adaptation
  and, 6-7
confidence training, 15
conflict
  of cultural tradition, 97
  interpersonal, 22, 23
  in multicultural teams, 17-25,
  26-27, 42-43
  of relative development, 96-98
  strategies for dealing with, 20-21,
  25-31
  in values, 85-102
conflict of cultural tradition, 97
conflict of relative development,
  96-98
co-opetition, 134
core values, 89, 91-93, 95, 98, 102
corporate culture. *See* company
  culture
corporate language policy,
  103-116
corporate structure, 65.
corporate values, 100. *See also*
  ethical behavior
corruption, 101. *See also* ethical
  behavior
cosmopolitan mind-set, 147
cross-cultural interactions, 12-13,
  22-24, 25
cross-cultural mistakes, 2, 12-13,
  22, 89
cultural buffers, 43-44

one-language policies, 103–116
openness, 64, 69–70
organizational culture, 1, 64, 68–69, 92, 93–95
organizational trust, 72–73

partners, in global innovation, 125–126
performance standards, 64
personal development, 64
persuasion, cultural attitudes toward, 77–78
physical aspects, of cultural intelligence, 4, 6
positive approach, to other cultures, 82–83
product development, 37–41
project management, 121–122

race, 48–49, 53, 54–57, 67
racism, 67, 70–71
Rakuten, 103–104, 110, 115, 116
regulatory environments, 97
relationship-centered societies, 131–132
relative development, conflict of, 96–98
repatriation, 139–140, 142, 150–152
rule-centered societies, 131–132

scheduling, 79, 123–124
self-efficacy, 6–7
sexism, 70–71
sexual harassment, 70–71
status, cultural attitudes toward, 136–138
stereotyping, 3, 75–76, 84

structural intervention, for multicultural teams, 21, 25, 26, 29–30
subcontractors, in global innovation, 125–126
subgrouping technique, in structural intervention, 29–30
subordination, 70–72
subsidiaries, differences between headquarters and, 44–45, 101
suppliers, ethics and, 100

tacit knowledge, 35–36, 118
teams
    dispersed, 118–119
    multicultural, 17–33, 38–45
technology, 126–127
time, attitudes toward, 79
translation, issues with, 41–42. *See also* communication
trust
    building across cultures, 6, 11, 78–79, 118–119, 124
    cognitive versus affective, 78–79
    on dispersed teams, 118–119, 124
    organizational, 72–73

Union Carbide, 90, 102

value conflicts, 85–102

Western culture, communication in, 18–19
workers. *See* employees
workforce diversity, 47–73

The most important management ideas all in one place.

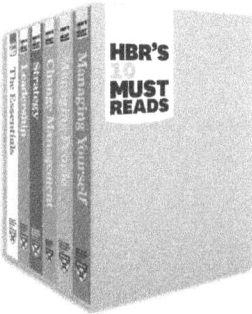

We hope you enjoyed this HBR's 10 Must Reads book. Now, you can get even more with HBR's 10 Must Reads Boxed Set. From books on leadership and strategy to managing yourself and others, this 6-book collection delivers articles on the most essential business topics to help you succeed.

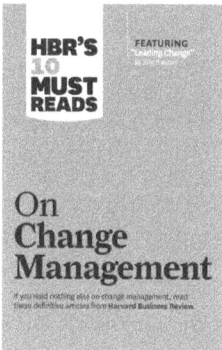

HBR's 10 Must Reads Series

The HBR's 10 Must Reads Series is the definitive collection of ideas and best practices on our most sought-after topics from the best minds in business.

- The Essentials
- Leadership
- Strategy
- Managing People
- Managing Yourself
- Collaboration
- Communication
- Making Smart Decisions
- Teams
- Innovation
- Strategic Marketing
- Change Management

www.ingramcontent.com/pod-product-compliance
Lightning Source LLC
Chambersburg PA
CBHW031417180326
41458CB00002B/410